A Guide to Shifting Your Consciousness

How We Heal and Transform Ourselves and Our World

Eileen Templin, LCSW, RYT

Copyright © 2011 by Eileen Templin

All rights to this book are reserved.

This workbook is for informational purposes only and is not a substitute for medical advice, diagnosis, or treatment.

ISBN 978-0-9967406-16

Printed in the U.S.A.

Dedication

This book is dedicated to Jennifer DeLoach, LCSW, the consummate therapist, teacher, mentor, breathwork retreat facilitator and healer. I have been graced by your love, wisdom, and healing; you have been the overriding agent of transformation in my life. This book could not have been written without the work you've enabled me to do. I am eternally grateful. Namaste.

TABLE OF CONTENTS

Acknowledgements

Introduction

Chapter One: Ego to Essence — Page 8
Who Are We, *Really*? And, What *Is* Self-realization?

Chapter Two: Thinking to Sensing — Page 17
The Role of the Body in Transformation

Chapter Three: Avoiding to Embracing — Page 25
The Necessity of Addressing Our Emotions and Our Unconscious

Chapter Four: Reacting to Choosing — Page 35
The Perceptual Lens through Which We See the World and Create Our Reality

Chapter Five: Past/Future to Present Moment — Page 43
The Primacy of the Mind and the Present Moment in Transformation

Chapter Six: Head to Heart — Page 52
The Heart as the Key and the Heart-Brain Connection

Chapter Seven: The Transformed Life — Page 61
Embodying and Living It

Epilogue: The Love of Power to the Power of Love — Page 68
The Global Shift and the Call to Sacred Activism

Recommended Reading and Resources — Page 72

About the Author — Page 76

Acknowledgements

This book is the result of numerous people who have touched my life and shared their wisdom, gifts, and selves with me. I would not have experienced transformation, or have gained the knowledge of how we heal without the influence of transpersonal psychotherapist, Jennifer DeLoach, LCSW. She has not only shared her wisdom and healing abilities with me and others, individually, she created a sacred circle of women who I have had the privilege to sit with, breathe with, and heal with for the past 20 years. It was through Jennifer's retreats that I was also exposed to the power of yoga. Words cannot convey the gratitude I have for the work she has done on herself that has enabled her to convey her gifts to others.

I've also had the good fortune to get to know Louise Goldberg, RYT 500, through my husband, Steve. Louise is a tremendously wise woman and a skillful yoga teacher. At a yoga retreat given by Louise and JoAnn Evans, RYT 500, I fell in love with yoga. As a result, I decided to embark upon the yoga teachers training and chose to do it through the Himalayan Institute. The experience at the Institute, and the teachings by the Institute staff, has also been life changing.

Of all the blessings in my life, none have been more wonderful and rewarding, personally and professionally, than that of my husband, Steven Templin, DOM. His knowledge, which is vast, and support have been instrumental in the writing and editing of this book. Steve has taught me about the body, and introduced me to somatic focusing and energy psychology. I've been the fortunate recipient of his healing work from which I've greatly benefited. He also ignited my interest in the information coming out of the new sciences. His encouragement, love, and sense of humor always uplift me.

My interest in the new neuroscience and the research coming out of the field of Positive Psychology was further developed through my work with an amazing group of people on the Liiv.com program development team. It was an honor and a joy to be part of such an inspiring and evolutionary project.

This book was also informed by the work of my psychotherapy clients over the years. I've had the privilege of being taught and inspired by them. Their courage, heart, and wisdom have deeply touched and stretched me. Finally, I want to acknowledge my parents, Bill and Wilma Frankland, whose deep faith, love, and support provided me the foundation for becoming all that I could be.

Eileen Templin
Lakeland, Florida
June 21, 2010

Introduction

This guide is offered as my way of sharing what I've learned and experienced in over 25 years of professional work as a social worker and psychotherapist, and my personal journey of healing and transformation over the years. I have attempted to distill the wisdom, process, and practices that for me form the core essentials of transformation. It is my hope that it will clarify, simplify, and support you in your own healing and evolving process.

What I know, and can tell you right up front, is this: Healing and transformation are possible. We can optimize our health and well-being. We can overcome loneliness, dis-connection, and polarization. We can fulfill our unique potential and become all that we can be. We can open our hearts and rewire our brains. And, we can find true happiness that is not dependent on externals, or the circumstances of our lives. I believe this is not only possible, but necessary at this juncture in the evolution of our species if we are to insure our survival.

This is a book about transformation, both personal and global. Whether you are seeking healing for a health issue, a mental, or emotional issue, relationship, or career issue, a spiritual issue, or to further evolve and grow as a human being, transformation is possible. I know because my "self" and my life have been transformed, and I've had the privilege of witnessing transformation in hundreds of clients.

Transformation is a process. It involves removing the obstacles to being the divine, embodied, and whole human being you were created to be and already are. This process involves making key shifts in consciousness that change how you perceive and relate to yourself, others, and the world; what we might call personal-paradigm shifts. And, as you make these shifts, you are also supporting the global shift in consciousness.

Our personal evolution is part of the larger evolution of consciousness, and is a prerequisite for global transformation. We are at a crossroads in terms of the future of our planet and our species. We do this work not only for ourselves but for the collective. Many of us are aware that we are living in a time of major evolutionary change; a global shift in consciousness is occurring. Some describe it as the birthing of the global heart, a movement from the "love of power" to the "power of love".

It is a death/rebirth process, so the old needs to die in order to birth the new. We see this in the many ways that our world is on the brink of destruction – finances, war and nuclear threat, and the environment, to name a few. However, at the same time, a growing momentum of people and institutions are embracing a new direction. We need these imaginal cells to coalesce into the new consciousness, which then manifests the new earth. Our personal work ensures that we are doing our part to achieve the critical mass that is needed to shift the collective consciousness. Many of us want this, but don't know how to make these shifts.

This book is offered as a guide and resource for doing your personal work. It synthesizes the ancient wisdom and practices of yoga, the insights and tools of transpersonal psychology, and cutting-edge research with its applications. This process will enable you to develop the skills to manage your mind, self-regulate your emotions, and turn on your mindbody's innate self-healing capacities. It's about moving toward optimal health and well-being, and becoming spiritually aligned, creatively enlivened, and heart-centered.

We all want to be healthy and happy. Despite all we now know about stress management and healthy lifestyles, vitality, health, and happiness often still elude us.
Why *do* optimal health and well-being remain elusive?
Why are contentment, peace, and joy difficult to attain and even harder to sustain?
Why does stress continue to zap our vitality?
Why are relationships so challenging, and too often feel depleting rather than uplifting?
Why do disturbing patterns keep recurring in our lives despite our attempts to rid ourselves of them?
Why do feelings of frustration, fear, and guilt weigh us down and drain our joy, passion, and light-heartedness?
Why do we so often sabotage our best efforts to change?

To answer these complex questions and address the riddles of health and well-being, a "shift" is needed. I am referring primarily to a paradigm shift; a shift to new patterns of awareness that change how we see ourselves and our world, how we relate to our bodies, thoughts, and feelings, and how we choose to act in our lives.

In the chapters ahead, we will explore a process that addresses the mind, emotions, body, and spirit to promote the healing of limiting beliefs, negative emotions, bodily constrictions, and energetic imbalances and blocks. All of these contribute to the root cause of mental and emotional "dis-ease," and ultimately of physical disease. You will learn ways to engage your body and its wisdom, restructure your brain, master your mind, open your heart and nurture your soul.

Each chapter addresses an essential shift that is needed and provides instruction in practices that enable you to make these shifts. The practices are noted by being preceded by the designation: ***EXERCISE*** so they stand out and are easy to find and return to. This approach incorporates ancient wisdom and modern psychology. To this base, is added current information from the fields of quantum physics, energy psychology, epigenetics, neuroscience, and neurocardiology.

These different perspectives give us a complementary roadmap to healing and transformation. The combination of tools and insights they provide can enable you to be healthier, more resourceful, and empowered in your life. Through my own personal work, and through my work with hundreds of clients as a psychotherapist, I have found this combination of perspectives profoundly helpful. My hope is that it will be as helpful to you. The key to its success lies in your willingness to do the practices. As many a great teacher has said: practice, practice, practice!

By sharing a bit of my story, I hope you will get a sense of how I came to write this book. As mentioned, I have been in the counseling field for over 25 years, of which the last 10 years I have been in private practice as a psychotherapist. My undergraduate degrees were B.A.s in both Social Work and Religious Studies, and my masters degree is in Clinical Social Work. I am also a certified Yoga teacher through the Himalayan Institute. My interests have always leaned toward psychology and spirituality, and I sensed early on that they were somehow inseparable. When I was introduced to Jungian psychology, my intuitive sense was confirmed, and the newer field of transpersonal psychology has further validated and brought a psycho-spiritual perspective into the mainstream dialogue.

Transpersonal psychology is the name for an umbrella of approaches that all share the belief that psychotherapy must address more than the ego/personality, as we are much more than our conscious minds. As I evolved as a therapist, I also became increasingly aware that to help people heal and achieve their true potential, we had to address the whole person: mind, emotions, body and spirit, or we risked missing an essential piece of the puzzle. I then explored various bodily-focused therapies and incorporated a holistic approach into my work with clients.

Along with my professional interests, personally, I have been a spiritual seeker my entire adult life. Having been raised in a Christian home with parents who modeled faith and devotion, I experienced the power of faith and had experiences of deep connection with God. Upon graduating from high school I went from an insulated, religiously dominated life in which I had not dated or even experimented with alcohol, to landing on the main campus of Penn State in the fall of 1969, and the world of "drugs, sex, and rock and roll."

The Social Work department at Penn State was in the Liberal Arts College. I ended up taking all my liberal arts electives in Religious Studies, which, in hindsight, I believe was an attempt to assuage all the guilt my newfound behaviors were evoking. In the process, I was exposed to a much broader understanding of religion and spirituality. I began to find it hard to believe that there was only one path to God, and did come to question some aspects of organized religion. That set the stage for my spiritual seeking, along with my desire to have a deeper and more direct experience of the divine.

Among other things, I have been a practicing meditator for the past 20 years, and have studied the mystical traditions of both the east and the west. Most recently, I fell in love with Raja Yoga and its ancient wisdom and practices. The yogi masters were among the original mystics who handed down the path to spiritual evolution. Carl Jung was greatly influenced by his study of the teachings and practices of yoga. He split from Freud because, among other things, he believed that an understanding of the psyche had to include a spiritual component, and that the healing process, itself involved a mystical understanding, and a spiritual experience. When asked if he believed in God, Jung responded "I don't believe, I know." I have healed and grown personally and professionally through my exposure to Jung's work and to yoga.

Finally, in terms of what lead up to the writing of this book, very exciting information from the fields of quantum physics, energy psychology, cellular biology, neuroscience, and neurocardiology are reconfiguring and expanding our knowledge in these areas; at times, turning conventional beliefs on their head. Much of the new science is confirming the role of consciousness in disease and in healing. And, the new science has produced evidence-based techniques that mesh with, enhance, and at times accelerate the desired results of the ancient practices.

The old paradigm that has separated spiritually and science is breaking down and a more integrative understanding is emerging. This book is a humble attempt to provide an overview and introductory understanding of some aspects of the ancient wisdom and practices of yoga, transpersonal psychology, and current science, all of which lead us toward higher consciousness, holistic healing, and optimal well-being.

This process promotes optimal well-being, in part, by facilitating the development of your unique potentials. As energetic beings, most all dis-ease starts on the energetic level and then manifests as stress, negativity, emotional imbalance, and/or physical limitation. Your thoughts and beliefs (conscious and unconscious), your moods and emotions, and your behaviors all effect, and are affected by how energy moves through your system. Learning how to attune to and activate the mind/body's healing wisdom, and remove the blocks in your energetic field unlocks the door to your unique potential. You have the factory equipment. You just need the owner's manual, some effective tools, and the willingness to practice, so you can become skillful in this process.

This "owner's manual" is informed by the three perspectives:
-the yogic tradition
-transpersonal psychology
-the new sciences

These perspectives share three common principles that are part of the foundation of their philosophy and practices. The first principle addresses our nature. The yogic traditions, Jungian psychology, and the sciences that we will be exploring, all have clear teachings about who we are, *essentially*. They all believe that we are both matter and energy/consciousness.

Whether we talk about our true nature as quantum particles/prana/life-force, or consciousness/pure awareness, or spirit/divinity, we are basically referring to the same essential truth: We are physical beings with a body, and psychological beings with an ego, or conscious personality, but we are also preemptively spiritual beings that are animated by, and infused with energy, consciousness, spirit. This energy also connects us with a larger field of creative intelligence known variously by such names as the Unified Field, Unmanifest, Source, God or Goddess, Great Spirit, etc.

Secondly, all three perspectives address the whole person. Yoga began as a path to spiritual evolution that incorporated practices that addressed the body, the breath, and the mind. Jungian psychology added a spiritual dimension to the process of exploring the mind and emotions. Jung also incorporated the body, another outcome of his study of yoga and the chakra system, which is the Indian version of the human energy system. Some Jungian therapists incorporate body work into their treatment. The latest research that we will be looking at, studies the mind-body connection and the role of consciousness, energy, and emotion in physical healing.

Finally, all three focus on the concept of self-regulation. They all believe that we have innate self-healing capacities, and that we are designed with the ability to restore balance to the system through an innate guiding intelligence and self-healing wisdom. This same intelligence guides and pulls us forward on our soul's evolutionary path. As David Richo states in his book, *The Power of Coincidence*, "We have three reliable and highly skilled healers-three graces-residing within us. The first is the inner physician-the grace of the body-who rushes to the scene of an accident. We cut a finger and he brings platelets to stop the bleeding....We also embody an inner psychologist-the grace of the psyche-who knows just how to help us with our emotional injuries...she brings tears of mourning... Finally...our inner priest, our spiritual guide-the grace of the soul-who knows the full itinerary of our journey through life and can offer the provisions it requires."

The inner guide supports us and guides us through our yearnings, dreams, intuitions, meditations, and synchronicities towards our soul's purpose and our destiny. In whatever manner we want to explain it, most people today are aware of spontaneous remissions, the placebo effect, remote healings, intention, and other indicators revealing our capacity to influence healing in ourselves and others. From Norman Cousin's *Anatomy of an Illness* and *Head First, The*

Biology of Hope, to the field of psychoneuroimmunology, to today's epigenetics, we now have the research that validates these capacities.

Embracing these three principles lays the foundation for our personal journey to healing and transformation. Upon this foundation will be the practices, tools and techniques that support us in making the necessary shifts.

To begin, the over-riding shift that all the other shifts support is the mindbody's shift from the defense/protection mode to the growth/healing mode. To put it simply, think of it this way: every cell of your body has basically two operational modes. The growth/healing mode gives the signal to the cell to do what it's supposed to do to support the organism's health and optimal functioning. The defense/protection mode signals the cell to shut down all functioning not necessary for survival and instead, focus on defense. Defense is necessary, but turns corrosive to our health and well-being when it is the primary mode of functioning.

In your body, this shift is experienced in a variety of ways, most notably by the autonomic nervous system in which the sympathetic nervous system initiates the stress response that puts you in the defense/protection mode. This mode automatically shuts down your body's ability to grow and heal; thereby obstructing your body's self-healing capacities. It is also a major drain on the entire system. The parasympathetic nervous system, on the other hand, initiates the relaxation response that puts you in the growth/ healing mode and supports healthy cell functioning and your self-healing capacities.

This shift from defense to growth is also experienced as a shift from an incoherent-heart rate-variability to a coherent-heart rate-variability, from limiting, negative beliefs, to expansive, affirming beliefs, and from disturbing, negative emotional states, to uplifting, positive emotional states. The practices and techniques we will be exploring are all designed to achieve and sustain these generative and life-enhancing shifts.

Another over-riding shift is from an outer, externally oriented focus, to an inner, internally oriented focus. One of the first prerequisites of this process is that we develop an inner life. Most of us are familiar with the old quotation "happiness is an inside job," and sense its truth. However, we have all been shaped by a culture whose predominant beliefs are diametrically opposed to that concept. In contrast, we have been taught that one's happiness is to be sought through externals - what one looks like, does, and has, along with the corollary that the more one has and does the better.

Surely, being accomplished and attaining material rewards are important, but we have focused on them often to the detriment of inner values and rewards. And often, less is more! We are beginning to re-evaluate this belief system as many of us experience what might be called an "existential" crisis - a crisis of meaning and purpose in our lives, despite having achieved and accomplished what we thought would bring us happiness and fulfillment. World affairs add to the sense of crisis. It's as if one day we step off the busy, demanding treadmill of our lives, look at ourselves, and begin to ask the deeper questions: Who am I, really? What do I want? Why am I here? What, ultimately, is important to me?

These are not questions that can be answered by looking outside ourselves, but require a looking inward. Outside guidance and resources are helpful along the way, but ultimately, the journey is an inward one. This journey, depicted for ages through myth and story, has been further delineated by mythologist, Joseph Campbell, as the "hero's or heroine's journey," and Jungians as the "process of individuation." Regardless of the particular path we take, the journey requires the development of an inner life. And just what does the development of an inner life involve: the commitment to set aside time on a regular basis to quiet our bodies; quiet our minds to access our larger, unconscious mind; to shift from our logical, analytical "left brain" to our more intuitive, symbolic "right brain"; to quiet our ego and attend to the voice of our soul.

Before closing the introduction to this book, I will offer the first practice.

EXERCISE

> If you are not already doing so, commit to a daily quiet time where you sit undisturbed and still, in silence, fully present to your inner experience – the thoughts, the mental images, the bodily sensations and emotional tones that arise... even if it's only for 5 - 10 minutes.
>
> Then hold on to your hat and let the journey begin! And don't forget, in this process, SHIFT HAPPENS!

This book comes out of my personal conviction that we must heal and transform ourselves, and our lives, so that we can be agents of transformation in our world now. I feel these shifts are necessary and timely. There is an imperative for personal and spiritual evolution. It is no longer a luxury. We on this planet have been on a very destructive path and time is running out. The global paradigm shift that is occurring offers the hope of salvation, but it's not guaranteed. We need that critical mass of people who have personally shifted their consciousness to a higher level and are living their lives accordingly, which, can then shift the collective consciousness to a higher level. My hope is that this book will motivate, encourage, and support you in doing just that.

My blessings to you and deepest wishes:
May this book and these practices bring you ease of well-being.
From the merits of these practices, may all beings be liberated from suffering.
May all beings be safe, happy and free.

Chapter One: Ego to Essence
Who Are We, Really? And What Is Self-realization?

The introduction laid the foundation for the shifts in consciousness that will be addressed in the remainder of this book. The process these shifts entail is the adventure of a lifetime. If we are to take this journey of healing and transformation, where do we begin? Perhaps by asking those very basic questions: who am I *really*, and what *do* I want? These questions lead to others such as: why am I here, and how do I fulfill my potential and give my unique gift to the world?

A number of years ago I heard the story of Peter Russell's answering machine. It goes something like this. If you called him and he was not available, what you heard on his message was: "This is not an answering machine, this is a questioning machine. Who are you and what do you want? And lest you think these are trivial questions, most people come into this world and go out of it without having answered either one". We would all do well to seriously ponder these questions. Take a moment right now to begin to do so.

EXERCISE

> Sit still and close your eyes. Take a nice relaxing breath. Now drop your attention into your heart and ask your heart: "Who am I?" As answers come, acknowledge them, and keep asking the question again and again. Allow the answers to rise up from ever deeper parts of yourself.
>
> Acknowledge all your roles (mother, son, grandparent, partner, step-parent, friend, teacher, lawyer, homemaker), as your sense of self is always connected to your roles. Let the roles go, and acknowledge the "doing" aspects of your identity (golfer, PTA mom, church elder, singer, volunteer, activist).
>
> Now, let those go as well. What remains when all of that is stripped away? Who is the "being" that remains? Take your time and allow yourself to be intrigued by your answers. Now or at a later time do the same thing with the question: "What do I want?"

Even if you feel you've answered these questions and are living your life accordingly, from time to time you've probably had the sense that you are less than you could be; the feeling that you and your life are not a reflection of your true potential. You know on some level that you can be more, but aren't. So, how do you become "all that you can be?" To understand your potential, you must go back to an understanding of who you are, *really* and *essentially*. We all tend to be identified with our personalities, or what we might call our egos. We also identify ourselves with our bodies. And certainly, they are both part of who we are. However, if we seek to know our essential nature, we must expand our perspective. Some say we are first and foremost energetic beings.

We often don't realize this because we are products of the Western cultural view that has historically believed that what we know and is "real" is based on the physical world, and what can be observed, experienced, and measured through the five senses. Thanks to quantum physics, we now know that consciousness (or mind) and matter, are just different vibrational levels of the same energy, making our minds and our bodies inseparable. We *are* much more energy than matter, and much more unconscious mind than conscious mind or ego. Despite what we now know, we still tend to identify predominantly with our physical form and ego.

In terms of our bodies, both the chakra energy system from India, and the meridian energy system from China, show us there is more to the body than meets the eye. There is an unseen energetic realm in the body that can be tapped into for healing and enhanced well-being. These expanded points of view give us options and a larger process for embracing our full potential. Whether we are talking about the unconscious psyche, or the unseen energetic realm of the body, we're referring to the same source of untapped potential. It is also referred to as the spiritual self or soul.

Beginning to identify with this larger part of us lays the foundation for the work we will be doing. This is our essential self, and it goes by many names: Higher self, true self, Buddha nature, Christ consciousness, witness, soul, and pure awareness. We begin with Essence awareness, the awareness that reflects who we really are. The first shift in consciousness we work toward is to increasingly identify with our Essential self, and through new choices and actions, realign our lives to reflect our new, enlarged identity.

Eastern philosophy and medicine have a long history of studying the human energy system. We will briefly discuss the Chinese meridian system when we look at the new field of Energy Psychology. We will mainly focus on the Yogic teachings of India. This ancient tradition has much to offer us today in terms of enhancing our happiness, supporting optimal well-being, and assisting us in evolving in consciousness. Yoga has been practiced in India for more than forty centuries. Historically, yoga was primarily associated with contemplative and meditative practices. Asanas, the stretches and postures, were not added until many years later. Somewhere around 200 B.C. the sage, Patanjali codified and presented the practices of yoga in the form of eight divisions, or limbs, which he described in the Yoga Sutras. These eight limbs have become known as Raja Yoga, the "royal" path, because they lead to the ultimate goal which is the realization of one's true nature. The eight limbs are:

Yamas – the 5 Restraints
Niyamas – the 5 Observances
Asana – Postures
Pranayama – Control and Expansion of Energy/Breathing Practices
Pratyahara – Sense Withdrawal

Dharana – Concentration
Dhyana – Meditation
Samadhi – Self-realization

The first division, which includes the first 5 limbs, is termed the external limbs of yoga, and involves the practices associated with one's relationship in the world, and with one's body, energy and senses. Concentration, meditation, and the ultimate goal, Samadhi or Self-realization, form the second division of the eight limbs, and are known as the internal or mental limbs of practice. Early on, postures tended to be seen as a means for developing the flexibility to sit comfortably for long periods of time in meditation. The masters found, however, that the asanas themselves opened energy channels, directed the flow of energy, and lead to some of the same spiritual states as meditation. The asanas, along with pranayama and pratyahara, came to be known as "Hatha Yoga". Pranayama is the breath training, and pratyahara is the withdrawal of the senses that occurs throughout the practice, especially in the final relaxation.

According to the 8 limbs of Raja Yoga, the goal of yoga is samadhi, or Self-realization. This involves the realization of our true nature as pure, ineffable, and eternal, and the discovery of the individual atman, or soul within us, through direct experience. The sages taught that there is one Divine reality whose light shines in every living thing, and that we can experience that same reality as our true Self. These ancient teachings lead to what has been referred to as the Perennial Philosophy by Aldous Huxley:
1. There is an infinite, changeless reality beyond the world of change.
2. This same reality lies at the core of every human personality.
3. The purpose of life is to discover this reality experientially.

This too lies at the heart of every mystical tradition: the seeking of direct experience with the Divine and the experience of our true self as one with the Divine… "I am That". As stated by Sandra Anderson and Rolf Sovic in *Yoga, Mastering the Basics*, "At the heart of Yoga is the message that every human being is, by nature, balanced and whole, and that this balanced inner self cannot be permanently destroyed or damaged. It is our inherent nature. Through Yoga it is said one may gradually be united with something higher, more subtle, more universal and more profound than we find in everyday consciousness – the pure nature of the Self."

So much of the "dis-ease" today is the result of what could be called a spiritual or existential crisis, a loss of meaning and purpose in life. We feel alone, cut off from others, ourselves, and from something larger than our selves – something mystical and awe inspiring. The practice of asana (postures), pranayama (breathing practices), pratyahara (sense withdrawal), and dharana (concentration) set the stage for the ability to meditate. The practice of daily meditation, which will be discussed in Chapter Five, is one of the best avenues to the realization of our true nature. This practice can heal our longing for a deeply satisfying spiritual connection, gracing our lives with a profound peace, and a knowing that we are deeply loved and connected to all that is.

Complementing the yoga teachings and practices, Jungian psychology further enhances our understanding of ourselves, our purpose, and our healing through working with both the conscious and unconscious mind. According to Carl Jung, within our unconscious is an Inner Center; Jung called it the Self with a large S. The Self, called by some the "God archetype" in the collective unconscious, is the regulating center of the psyche, responsible for fulfilling the blueprint for life. From this synthesizing center, the life force within us seeks to manifest our true essence: to bring to fruition the unique, authentic, and whole human being that we were created to be.

This same process occurs throughout nature. Within the tiny acorn is the blueprint for the intelligence to become a giant oak tree. In nature, this process is automatic. In humans, however, this process must occur through the ego and requires that the ego become conscious of more than itself. Why is this?

Kathleen Brehony, Ph.D., depicts this process succinctly in her book, *Awakening at Midlife*. "All is Self at birth: the latent ego is in complete correspondence with the Self. Over time, however, the ego begins to separate from the Self... in the course of development the ego becomes increasingly differentiated from the Self. This is as it should be, for the tasks of the 1st half of life require the establishment of a strong ego. Establishing a sense of identity, developing a career, entering into a significant relationship, giving birth and raising children, contributing to the society, and becoming independent of one's family of origin all depend on the establishment of an ego-identity."

The formation of a sense of identity is the developmental task of adolescence (Erickson's Identity vs. Role Confusion), and serves to prepare one for the tasks of adulthood mentioned above. Even though the development of a strong ego is healthy and necessary, it thwarts the inner developmental process of the Self. The ego is developed, in a sense, at the expense of our Self. We become dissociated from our true self, and we develop a partial self - what Jung called a persona. This persona, the face we show the world, serves us, but is also very limited and often fear-based. That is why we so often experience ourselves as much less than we know we can be. Our ego/persona is the smallest part of who we are. In comparing the ego to the unconscious, some Jungians have used the analogy of a cork (ego) floating in the ocean (unconscious).

By mid-life, however, the psychological priorities shift. It is the time for our Self to re-emerge. The task reserved for the second- half of life is what the Jungians refer to as the process of individuation. The ego must confront the unconscious and begin to dialogue with the Self. It is time to get back to the goal of the Self, which is psychological wholeness and authenticity. This is the journey to our Self and what Jung referred to as the healthy ego/Self axis. We become completed, whole, and self-actualized, or as Maslow described it: becoming everything that one is capable of becoming.

This process initiates what I refer to as the "dance of the ego and the Self." Through this dance, the ego becomes healthy, but also progressively subordinated and aligned with the Self. The first-half of life is the reflection or manifestation of our ego; the second-half of life is the process of manifesting our ego/Self. Adolescence initiates the manifestation of our ego, whereas mid-life initiates the manifestation of our Self. Both are crises of identity, one based on the ego, and formulated through our roles, the other based more on the Self apart from our roles. This process points the way to living outside the confines of our ego, and to forming a relationship between our ego and our Self through integrating the conscious and unconscious mind. We'll be addressing this in greater length in subsequent chapters.

Finally, in terms of the new science, quantum physics has turned Newtonian physics on its head. The old paradigm saw matter as the ultimate and essential reality. Quantum physics suggests that consciousness is not the by-product of evolution, but the common ground of existence. Consciousness is the essential reality that ultimately turns into time, space, and matter. Scientists found that atoms, the basis of matter and everything in the physical universe, are not solid but rather are composed of fluctuations of energy and information, moving at lighting speed around huge "empty" spaces. Atoms are actually a void of pure, vibrant consciousness, and potentiality, that can become information, energy, and ultimately matter. **We are in our essence pure consciousness**.

This realm of infinite possibilities and pure consciousness has been called the Unified Field, the Unmanifest, the Ground of Being, or simply, the Field. Lynne McTaggert's book, *The Field,* reviews much of the latest research on these topics. She states, "Living consciousness somehow is the influence that turns the possibility of something into something real. The most essential ingredient in creating our universe is the consciousness that observes it." This is science's way of describing the Self by saying we are essentially consciousness and that the mindbody is imbued with, and immersed in, this Field of intelligent energy.

Bruce Lipton, PhD, whose work will be discussed in Chapter Five, is a cutting edge cell biologist whose research has integrated quantum physics with cell biology. In an interview of Lipton by George Noory of Coast to Coast AM radio, (February of 2005), Lipton talked about cells and identity. He shared that after twenty years of cell research, in 1985, one night at 1:59 AM, he had an epiphany, that lead him to rewrite the definition of cell membrane, and in that moment, he claims that his entire life changed.

The new definition was that the cell membrane is a liquid crystalline semi-conductor with gates and channels. When he thought about it, he knew the definition sounded familiar. Then, he saw his book on computers, and looking in it, found that the definition of a computer chip was virtually the same. He realized that the cell membrane was an "organic information chip" that reacted to signals from the environment, and that these signals are what activated the cell, not the genes or DNA. Knowing that cells have their own identity, he saw that it was the cell membrane that had a set of protein antennae unique to each person that received signals from the outside. The antennae were the receivers, and the identity actually came from outside the cell. Thus, Lipton says, our identities are linked to an exterior "field of energy" that is sending the signals. Now, from a biological perspective, one could say our true identity, or Self, is linked to what quantum physics calls the Field.

Knowing all of this, how do we then make the shift from ego to Self/Essence? It starts with Essence awareness and the direct experience of our essential nature, which is awareness, itself. The yogis and mystics are the masters of this process. A practice that helps facilitate this shift is mindfulness. We begin by learning to activate what is called "witness consciousness." To get a sense of what this is, I will guide you through a beginning experience called "present moment awareness."

This exercise guides you to a heightened awareness of your sensory experience through focused attention on sights, sounds, and sensations. The intense, focused awareness quiets the mind. When the mind quiets, it rests in the present moment and there is stillness. This experience is very calming and peaceful. It also sets the stage for you to be more aware of your thoughts and feelings as they arise, so you can work with the ones that detract from your well-being and nurture those that enhance your well-being.

EXERCISE

> Read through the description. Then take a few moments to go back through the description and experience it.
>
> Sit with your spine straight and your arms and legs uncrossed. Take a few nice, deep breaths and quiet your mind.
>
> Now look around you and become intensely aware of the **sights** you see. Notice the colors, shapes and textures of the objects around you in an increasingly focused way. See them as if for the first time.
> While aware of the sights around you, also become aware of the **sounds**. Just listen to the sounds in your environment as if you have never really heard them before.
> While aware of the sights and sounds, also become aware of **bodily felt sensations**. Feel your clothes where they touch your body, the coolness of the AC or the warmth of the sun on your skin. Really look, listen and feel the bodily felt sensations in this moment.
> After several minutes of doing this, observe how you are feeling.

In this short exercise, you have just experienced your sense of sight, sound, and touch, and you were aware of them as you were experiencing them. Who is the part of you that was aware of your experiences? It is "the Witness," your capacity for awareness that transcends the conscious mind. As Richard Moss, M.D. explains in his book *The Mandala of Being*, "When we are aware of hunger...or anger, the aspect of us that is aware is not itself hungry... or angry. It is a higher consciousness that resides within us and is always there. This awareness has been called our true self and is the "being" in human being. Who we are in our essence is ineffable consciousness, not reducible to any thing."

In activating the Witness, you open to a more spacious awareness. Mindfulness is the ability to activate the witness and be aware of your own inner experience, whether it is thoughts, emotions, memories, images, or bodily sensations. So often, it is these barely conscious thoughts, images, etc. that create your "dis-ease" and compromise your well-being. When you can step back and observe them, rather than be hijacked by them, they have much less power over you. That's freedom. Then you get to be in charge and choose how you want to respond, giving you much more say in how you feel. There are many versions of the practice of mindfulness. The following is a beginning practice. If this is new to you, it is helpful to practice it while sitting still.

EXERCISE

Begin by sitting quietly and focusing your attention on your breath. Notice your breath as it goes out and goes in, out and in. Keep observing your breath. As you do this, thoughts, sensations and/or feelings will pop into your mind. Instead of getting caught up in them and going off on a tangent, as a thought, feeling, or sensation arises, you do the following:

Recognize: Observe it from the Witness, bringing your attention to it, and then name it (This is anger, critical thought, pleasant memory, a pain in my leg, etc.).

Accept: Welcome and accept the thought or feeling without judging it or deciding to like or dislike it. Rather than wanting more of it or to get rid of it, you just be with whatever it is in an open, curious, and compassionate way.

Dis-identify: Realize that you are **not** the thought or feeling; you are the Observer of it. This helps you to dis-identify with it, which makes it easier to then release it and let it go.

Statements that can help you dis-identify with a thought, feeling or sensation are: "Here am I experiencing _____ (critical thoughts)", which comes from Richard Moss, M.D. Or, "A wave of _____ (anxiety) is trying to overtake me", which comes from Roberto Assagioli, M.D., in his book *Psychosynthesis*.

This introductory practice is ideally done as a seated meditation for 15 to 20 minutes; part of a daily quiet time. As you develop this skill, the practice can be greatly expanded. Resources for information on Mindfulness, and the practice of it, can be found in the Recommended Reading Section of the book.

Mindfulness is also a practice you can take into your life to become more conscious, present in the moment, and happy. As life happens, instead of just reacting, the practice allows you to unplug from automatic pilot by recognizing, accepting, and dis-identifying from whatever you are experiencing. You then have the ability to *choose* how you wish to respond. This opens the door to self-regulation and personal empowerment. This practice is so powerful because you develop the ability to add a qualitative dimension to whatever you are experiencing. You add the wisdom, compassion, and unconditional love of the heart.

Dan Siegel, M.D. in his book, *The Mindful Brain*, talks about mindfulness as an attuned relationship with oneself in which we "feel felt." He uses the acronym COAL to describe mindful awareness: we approach our here and now experience with curiosity, openness, acceptance and love. Siegel reports that the practice of mindfulness, due to this process of attunement, promotes the growth of fibers in the prefrontal cortex of the brain, which leads to balanced self-regulation, and a process called neural integration that enables self-understanding, and an innate sense of well-being.

Similarly, Richard Moss refers to "sacred attention." Moss states, "The practice of sacred attention is a deepening of mindfulness in which we focus on the quality of attention we offer ourselves as we notice our thoughts, reactions and feelings. We offer our attention with a quality of exquisite receptivity and tenderness, no matter what we're experiencing and in so doing transform the experience. This intimate viewing of our selves by our awareness is the most fundamental of all relationships. In it we create the possibility of a conscious, empathetic connection between me (ego/self) and our Essence (Self)."

This presence (Self) can be our trusted friend and inner companion. **And, in so doing, we learn how to take ourselves into our own hearts with compassion and acceptance. This is a truly transformative practice. Our ability to move from judging ourselves and our thoughts, feelings, and reactions to acceptance, and then to giving unconditional love to ourselves is an essential component of the process of deep healing and transformation.** Through experiencing witness consciousness and the Self, we come to know our true nature, and expand our personality beyond the confines of our egos.

Once we've established who we are, essentially, the work is to identify more and more with the Self, and to develop the self-Self relationship. Only then, will our identity include the totality of who we are, and we open to being guided by this unbounded, creative intelligence. We *are* spirit, psyche, and body which are ultimately inseparable, but which do function independently; all affect our mental, emotional, physical, and spiritual well-being. Therefore, we must work with each of these aspects of ourselves, if we are to become whole and transformed. The process becomes a dance of effort and grace. The effort we put forth through our practices, leads to the grace of a shift in consciousness. As taught by Swami Rama, the message of the sages is very clear: "Develop a set of practices that is appropriate for the conditions of your life, and then devote yourself to that practice with a happy heart. There is no higher joy in life".

The first practice that is suggested, and which supports the shift from ego to Essence, is the practice of mindfulness. As part of a daily quiet time, start with 10 minutes of sitting quietly and focusing your attention on your breath. As thoughts, sensations, or feelings arise, recognize and name them; non-judgmentally accept them; finally, dis-identify with them by noticing that you are not the thought or sensation, but the awareness that is observing it. Let go of it and return to focusing on your breath.

It is important to remember not to judge yourself when your mind wanders. That is what the mind does. Just notice it and gently return to the breath. With time, lengthen the duration of your practice, so that it lasts at least 20 minutes. When you experience yourself as the Witness, as pure awareness, you are experiencing your Essence. Allow yourself to be awed by who you really are! Mindfulness practices are instrumental in many of the shifts we will be exploring.

Chapter Two: Thinking to Sensing
The Role of the Body in Transformation

Having said in Chapter One, that we need to see ourselves and identify with more than our egos and our bodies, I now want to emphasize the importance of our bodies in this transformational process. We must not ignore the critical role of our relationship to our physical bodies. We are products of a culture that has created a split between our psycho-spiritual nature and pursuits, and our bodily life. The body is often portrayed as being separate from the mind, of less value, and ignored as a consequence. As a result, many of us live from the neck up and feel disconnected from our bodies. We live in our heads, thinking, thinking, thinking, and have lost touch with the ability to experience, and be guided by the *felt sense* of our bodies. That is why the second shift we are addressing is the shift from thinking to sensing, from mind-bound beings to embodied beings. Ultimately, we want a balance of both.

The yogis had an inclusive view of our physical nature. Even though their goal was spiritual evolution, and they taught at length about not being a slave to the desires of the senses and body, they also knew that the body was an essential component of spiritual practice. The ultimate work was the management of the mind, but they knew that required addressing the body. Enlightenment required working with the body, the breath, and the mind. A limber and pain free body enabled one to sit for longer periods of time in meditation, and pain and ill health can become consuming, which distracts us from, and inhibits our ability to focus on spiritual pursuits. On the other hand, a healthy body and proper breathing, which controls the flow of energy in the body, both set the stage for a quiet and tranquil mind. The yogis knew that the body, breath, and mind are also the keys to optimal health.

Many of us are aware of the health benefits of Hatha Yoga. It incorporates stretches and postures, breathing practices, and systematic relaxation, all of which sets the stage for meditation. Entire books have been written on the benefits of yoga, which is far beyond the scope of this book. If you would like to learn more about the health and healing benefits of yoga, I recommend the book *Yoga As Medicine,* by Timothy McCall, M.D. I will share only a small piece of this body of information. Yoga promotes physical, psychological, and spiritual health through what I call the "4 D's". They are Diet/Lifestyle, Digestion, Detoxification, and De-stress.

I think it goes without saying that diet and exercise are two of the primary determiners of health and quality of life, especially as we age. This is as true for psychological health as physical health. People have actually alleviated depression and anxiety through changes in diet and exercise. The significance of moving the body, making it more supple and flexible, and relaxing it, will become increasingly evident as we continue. In my opinion, yoga is one of the greatest health and anti-aging practices there is.

The yoga tradition of Swami Rama recommends daily walking, along with a yoga practice, as well as, cleansing practices and dietary guidelines. Yoga practices are known to improve digestion and elimination. If your digestion is off, even if your diet is good, the nutrients will not be broken down and absorbed into your body. This also means you will not produce the neurochemicals that are a byproduct of digestion. Neurochemicals play a major role in your mood states. If your digestion is not efficient, it can set the stage for a clinical depression. If you are not properly eliminating, toxins are emitted into your system. Toxins and stress are now believed to be major causes of disease. Yoga supports the natural detoxification of the body. It facilitates detoxification through increased respiration and circulation, the compression and massaging of organs, and enhanced lymphatic drainage. Finally, yoga has a centuries-old record of effective stress reduction that we have the science to now validate.

Stress deserves some additional attention as it is such a factor in health and well-being. The Center for Disease Control now acknowledges the critical role of stress in disease. Many of us are experiencing chronically high levels of stress in our lives. This not only leads to dis-ease and disease, but drains our energy and vitality. We know the stress response is triggered by a perceived threat to the organism. When triggered, our bodies do two things instinctively and immediately: our breath is suspended or our breathing becomes very shallow, and we tense and tighten our muscles. When this is done repeatedly, our bodies develop what is called "character armor" whereby our bodies lock in this muscular tension and it becomes the way our body is held. The tension can be in our eyes, jaw, neck and shoulders, chest, abdomen, hands, back – just about anywhere. We then also tend to be habitually-shallow breathers.

This 'armoring" is initiated to protect us, but it ends up becoming part of a feedback loop to the brain that keeps the stress response activated. If the muscles are tense, it must mean there's a threat. And since most of the perceived threats nowadays are psychological, the tension and shallow breathing serves to keep our emotions repressed. It's been said that our bodies hold our wounds along with our wisdom. Physical and psychological healing, as well as, well-being requires that our bodies release the tension open up the breath.

The breath is usually something we take pretty much for granted even though we would not stay alive long without it. However, other than the fact that it keeps us alive, why would we be interested in our breathing? Well, what if we were to see that the quality of our breathing was directly connected to the quality of our lives? Would it make it more interesting if the breath and how we breathed could create vitality, mental clarity, emotional stability, and a greater sense of peace in our lives? Most of us would probably say it would. In fact, the most common inhibitors of greater well-being, such as, stress, fatigue, mental fogginess, worry, and headaches, have been relieved through the practices of breath awareness and breath training.

So how does the breath play such an important role in our well-being? The answer to that lies in understanding more about the breath. The breath carries oxygen and nitrogen into our bodies which nourishes our cells and allows them to function properly. It also disposes of waste products in the cells, thereby, cleansing and detoxifying our cells. This on-going out and in of the breath maintains the balance of cleansing and nourishing necessary to sustain our lives and to keep us healthy. But the breath does not only carry oxygen, it carries prana, the life force or energy that animates our bodies. Much dis-ease and disease starts on the energetic level as blocks or imbalances to the flow of energy in the body, and then manifests as physical or psychological symptoms. Breath training allows us to channel and balance the flow of this subtle energy, which is responsible for the maintenance of all the body's functions.

Correct breathing calms and focuses the mind, calms the nervous system decreasing stress and anxiety, creates a sense of well-being, and is both restful and revitalizing. How then, do you make sure that you are breathing correctly? You start with practices that help you gain breath awareness, and then practices that enable you to train your breath. The first step is to cultivate a sustained awareness of your breath as it flows out and in.

EXERCISE

> Take a few moments and read over, and then do the following:
>
> Focus your awareness on your breath. Notice the breath as it moves out and in, out and in. Feel your breath through the tips of your nostrils. Take a number of breaths just focusing on the sensation of the breath in your nostrils as you inhale and exhale. Notice the temperature of the breath. Is it cool or warm? You may notice that the breath feels cool and dry on the inhale and warm and moist on the exhale. Is your breath rough or smooth? Notice the inhalation and the exhalation – is one longer than the other? Are there pauses between them?
>
> Just observe, without judgment, how you are breathing right now. In this practice you are activating the witness consciousness I introduced in the last chapter, which allows you to observe and bring awareness to your breath. Continue to focus your awareness on your breath and when your mind wanders, gently bring it back to the breath.

We focus and hold our attention on the breath so we can observe it and then begin to shape it. The goal is breathing that is deep, smooth, even, and without sound or pause between the inhales and exhales.

"The word *BREATH* implies more than the physical act of drawing air in and out of the lungs. Breath is the junction point between mind, body, and spirit. Every change of mental state is reflected first in the breath and then in the body"
Deepak Chopra

The next step is learning to breathe diaphragmatically. The following instructions will guide you in diaphragmatic breathing.

EXERCISE

> As you inhale, lift the arms over your head and hold them there, clasping the palms together. Although you are holding the stretch, do not hold your breath.
>
> Continue to breathe out and in without pause, maintaining your awareness of the breath. If you soften your abdomen, you will feel a dramatic expansion and contraction there and at the sides of the rib cage. Both expand on the inhale and relax on the exhale. These movements are the result of deeper breathing.
>
> When you are ready, exhale and lower your arms. After 7 or 8 breaths settle into normal breathing.

When we breathe more deeply and diaphragmatically, we turn off the sympathetic nervous system that initiates the stress response, and we turn on the parasympathetic nervous system, which initiates the relaxation response and self-healing. We can reduce anxiety, and even back down a panic attack by learning to work with our breath. There are many breathing practices that can be used to move energy in the body, enhance our health, and alter our consciousness. You can refer to the Recommended Reading and Resource section where you will find resources for additional information and practice instructions. Breath training is also offered as part of the yoga classes at many yoga centers.

Breath awareness leads to body awareness. With body awareness, we again activate witness consciousness to observe and connect with bodily felt sensations, and with our own bodies. Forming a conscious connection with our own bodies is an essential part of healing and transformation. As stated earlier, muscular tension needs to be released for repressed material to become conscious and energy to be unblocked. Jack Lee Rosenberg, PhD, Marjorie Rand, PhD and Diane Asay explain the importance of this in their book *Body, Self & Soul*, in which they state:

"The sum of early life experiences is known as the Primary Scenario... This collection of experiences is what formed our basic characters... By *character*... we mean the fixed muscular patterns, emotional responses, and belief systems held in the body. The child, sealing off his unsatisfied pain, tightens his body to keep the pain from penetrating too deeply. Contacting the blockages..., relaxing the tensions that produced them, and thereby releasing the energy to flow freely, allows the emergence of the stunted Self buried within."

In this process, we use our bodies as an entry point to explore, feel and release blocked energy and emotions. We have the chance to transform personal fears, limitations, and self-concepts. We do this by consciously attuning to our own bodies, and through doing practices such as, breath and body awareness, breath training, movement, and deep relaxation. A simple practice follows.

EXERCISE

This practice starts with you lying down at a place and time where you can be undisturbed. Clothing needs to be comfortable so that nothing is restricting the body. Arms and legs are uncrossed. Cushions can be used under knees or neck for comfort. Read the exercise over several times to become familiar with it and then guide yourself through it. Better yet, record it so you can play it back for yourself.

> Settling into a comfortable position, begin to let your body relax... feel yourself supported by the floor (or bed) beneath you. Feel the weight of your body sinking into the floor and tell your entire body-mind it can relax, release and let go.
>
> Quieting the mind and turning inward... letting go of all your thoughts and all your cares. Letting go of all you did today and all that's scheduled for tomorrow... this time is for you, a time to be fully present to yourself and your body.
>
> Now focusing your attention on the breath...notice the breath as it flows out and in... out and in. Feel the natural rhythm of your own breath...feel it flowing out and then flowing in. Now gently begin to deepen the breath, allowing the exhalation to get longer and the inhalation to get longer...and imagine that with every exhalation you are releasing all toxins, all tension, and all negativity...and with every inhalation you are bringing in prana, energy and nourishment to every cell in your body...every exhales cleanses, carrying away wastes and fatigue...every inhale nourishes, drawing in fresh energy and a sense of well-being.
>
> Moving your attention from your breath to your body, begin to scan your body with your awareness. Feel your whole body... now feel your head and face, softening your eyes and loosening your jaw... feel your neck and shoulders, dropping your shoulders... feel your whole spine,... now feel your arms, hands, fingers and fingertips, letting the hands go limp... feel your chest, solar plexus and belly, softening the belly... feel your legs, feet, toes and tips of the toes.
>
> Now with your mind's eye, scan your body from head to toe for any remaining tightness or tension...if there is any, then take the inhalations to that area and release the tension on the next few exhalations. When ready, gently bring your attention back to the room you are in, make small movements to reawaken the body and slowly sit up.

This practice helps to bring you into your body, relax it, and begin to sensitize you to felt senses in your body. There are many forms of systematic relaxation that can be explored. There are CDs with guided relaxation that you can use, and relaxation is a part of most yoga classes. We will also be looking at another very important practice called somatic focusing later in this chapter.

Carl Jung also believed that the body must be addressed, and that the body was part of the process of individuation. Jung stated: "The Self has its roots in the body". The sense of the Self arises from the depths of the body and our repressed psychic material is rooted in the body. If so, how do we bring these unconscious aspects of ourselves to consciousness if we do not address the body?

Jung called the subtle body, the somatic unconscious. Our work is to bring consciousness to the body and it will do the rest. It is part of our self-healing capacities. Marion Woodman states: "The soul, which is embedded in the body, needs to be released through an increased suppleness and consciousness in the body, so that Spirit may be more and more embodied." She would not do analysis with a patient if they were not also doing some form of bodywork, such as yoga, acupressure, massage, or some form of energy work.

J. Conger writes in *Jung and Reich: The Body as Shadow*, "A body uninformed by mind and spirit may be given over to instinctual life, but a mind uninformed by the body loses its judgment... blunders and retreats. Without the body, the wisdom of the larger self cannot be known." Various forms of body psychotherapy have been around since Jung. Often they involve some form of subtle touch which is believed to induce self-regulation in the mindbody. One example is a method of subtle touch called Calatonia.

Somatic Focusing is a practice and therapeutic tool that is a bodily-oriented form of self awareness which has tremendous healing potential. The concept and practice of what I am referring to as somatic focusing, has been around for a long time and comes in many versions with varying names. I am presenting here a brief snapshot of this practice. The Resource section will give you sources for additional information. The most well known expert and originator of focusing, as it is known today and used therapeutically, is Eugene Gendlin, Ph.D., from the University of Chicago. He has written the books, *Focusing* and *Focusing Oriented Psychotherapy*.

Somatic Focusing incorporates both mindfulness and body awareness. It is a method of body awareness that has you attune to "felt senses" in your body. Felt senses have been described as feelings, body sensations, and things you have a sense of in your body, but cannot yet put into words. They can be a subtle sense of pressure, tightness, tingling, or just an area of your body that wants your attention. Your head and your body both know things about you. And, your body tries to tell you what it knows through these felt senses. Your body has an innate wisdom and an amazing capacity for self-healing, which you can tap into through the practice of Somatic Focusing. The practice goes as follows:

EXERCISE

> Sit in a comfortable position with arms and legs uncrossed. Take a few nice relaxing breaths. Close your eyes and bring your awareness into your body.
>
> Scan your body as done in the body awareness exercise and pay attention to whatever is going on in your body or calling for your attention... Notice even subtle sensations... Ask yourself, "What inside me, feels like it most needs to be listened to right now?"
>
> Take time to notice what it is... Notice where in your body you feel it (in my chest)... Notice how it feels in your body... (like a heavy weight is on my chest). See if you can be with it in a gentle, curious, non-judgmental way... If it doesn't feel good, see if you can give it some caring presence as you notice how it feels. Just keep staying with it.
>
> Don't think about it, stay with the body feel of whatever is there, waiting for something to come...a word, a feeling, a memory, an image...allowing your inner story to unfold.
>
> If nothing comes, don't worry; your attention is enough. Your body's wisdom will sort it out. If you feel a shift, notice the difference in how it feels. Take some time to be with it.

Through this practice, you learn to scan your body and pay attention to felt senses. Knowing the body's wisdom will unfold, and energy will shift, if you just give it your sustained attention. Also, when you are aware that something is bothering you, just drop into your body to feel where in your body you experience, or hold the disturbance. Then, notice even the subtlest of sensations that go with the "body feel" of whatever you are experiencing. Again, you give the felt sense your gentle, curious, non-judgmental attention allowing anything to come... a word, image, memory, feeling, bodily shift... opening to the wisdom and self-healing of your body. If something comes, just stay with the body feel of whatever it is and give it your caring, gentle attention.

This is where the similarity to mindfulness and sacred attention comes in. No matter what comes up or you are experiencing, try to embrace it and receive it as a gift, rather than want it to go away, even if it's disturbing or painful to you. Instead, you give it your gentle, accepting, and loving attention. In so doing, it is transformed and the energy around it freed up. This practice can be done as part of your daily quiet time to explore whatever needs attention at that time, or it can be used when something has come up and you want to shift it. Somatic focusing turns on your self-healing capacities, and facilitates the shift from being in your head, analyzing, to being in your body, sensing. **Sensing produces a**

shift in the somatic unconscious, making the practice much more transformational as the conscious mind tends to keep reformulating different versions of the same old patterns. It takes the unconscious to come up with a truly new and creative solution or option. The subtle body, or somatic unconsciousness, like the unconscious mind, can do that.

In terms of the newer research, much of it has been influenced by quantum physics and the inseparable mind-body link. Many of the new insights into consciousness have come from the study of the body. We will see this when we talk about the information that has come out of the fields of cellular biology and neurocardiology. The relatively new field of energy psychology uses the energy system of the body to stabilize and self-regulate emotions and mood, and it's done in part by tapping on meridian points on the body. This will be discussed more in a later chapter.

Candice Pert, the research scientist who discovered neuropeptides, and authored *The Molecules of Emotion*, states that the body is the subconscious mind. It's also been said that the body is the condensation of consciousness. Christiane Northrupt, M.D. begins her book, *Women's Bodies, Women's Wisdom* with the statement, "Consciousness creates the body." If that is true, might we consider bodily rigidity, pain, and tension as revealing rigidity, judgment, or limitation in consciousness? If so, then when the body opens, consciousness opens. And as Eckert Tolle states: "Do not turn away from the body, for within it is concealed the splendor of your essential and immortal reality. Underneath the body you see lies the invisible inner body, the doorway into Being. Through the inner body you are inseparably connected to the Divine. The more consciousness you direct into the inner body, the higher its vibrational frequency becomes." This requires not only a conscious connection to the body, but also a focused awareness on and into the body.

So why is it so important that we not ignore the body? Because it not only supports enhanced health and well-being through its self-regulating and healing capacities, it is an instrumental part of the much needed transformation of consciousness. At this point in the evolution of consciousness, we are being asked to not only become more spiritually evolved, but to reflect that inner development in all our actions in the world. We are to become the divine, *embodied*, whole human being we were created to be, and to inhabit and love our bodies. To do this, we must be grounded in the physical and attuned to our bodies. **For it is through the sensory experience of our bodies that we connect directly to the energetic realm of the Divine**. There are many paths to coming into our bodies. I have touched on a few that I have found to be highly effective. Find *the one or ones* that work for you and commit yourself to it. It is a shift that can change your life.

Chapter Three: Avoiding to Embracing
The Necessity of Addressing Our Emotions and Our Unconscious

In the last chapter, we talked about the importance of establishing a conscious connection with our bodies. In addition to attending to our bodies, the other aspects of ourselves we cannot ignore are our emotions and our unconscious. We have already begun this process as we have looked at the somatic unconscious or subtle body when I introduced the practices of body awareness and somatic focusing in Chapter Two. In this chapter, we will explore the unconscious mind and the power of unconscious beliefs and emotions.

The unconscious mind and the somatic unconscious really cannot be differentiated, as they are two ways of describing the same unconscious terrain. I will be presenting additional practices that access this unconscious material. I believe it was Einstein who said that we can never solve a problem at the same level of consciousness that created it. So we are exploring ways to access and work with a higher, larger consciousness for healing, transformation, and optimal well-being. That is what most of the practices and tools I am presenting in this book are designed to do.

We live in a culture that tends to value "thinking and doing" more than "feeling and sensing." And, our basic instincts are to seek pleasure and avoid pain so that anything that is painful or uncomfortable, we often want to avoid. This certainly applies to our emotions, and is seen in the way we like to "sweep them under the rug". Our religious or spiritual values can also cause us to want to avoid disturbing emotions related to an experience and go right to an intellectual understanding and acceptance of it, so we can feel loving and more evolved.

For example, in relation to our childhoods, when we make statements such as, "I know my parents did the best they could at the time," without having processed our emotions, both conscious and unconscious, related to those experiences, we may think we understand and accept our parents and home life. However, we may find old feelings being triggered and resurfacing, or being acted out unconsciously. To achieve true acceptance of our experiences and true liberation from our pasts, we need to address the emotions. It's been said that we can't change the past, but we need to deal with the feelings we're still carrying around with us today about the past. If not, it is a major obstacle to our healing and transformation.

So what are these emotions we are not to ignore? Emotions can be thought of as energy; "energy in motion," we might say. As energetic beings, energy has to move for our developmental processes to proceed. All energy wants to move and express itself. Blocked energy disrupts the process and ultimately turns the energy against us, producing many of our most common physical and psychological complaints. All blocked or trapped energy wants to be released. Not feeling our emotions, which means they are suppressed, is one of the main ways we block energy. Unfortunately, none of us gets through childhood and life without having to psychologically repress, and hold in our bodies all kinds of emotions that otherwise would be too overwhelming or painful for our ego's to tolerate. Therefore, our life force and energy get blocked as our emotions get suppressed or repressed (unconscious suppression).

We use psychological defenses such as denial, rationalization, intellectualization, and minimization, as well as, bodily defenses which we have called "character armor" to repress threatening emotions like fear, sadness, hopelessness, anger, guilt, and shame. Psychologically, our second line of defense against feelings is compulsivity or addiction. Our tendency to stay busy even to the point of exhaustion reflects our need to unconsciously distance ourselves from experiencing our own genuine emotions. As we engage in bodywork, tension is released from the body and energy begins to flow allowing suppressed emotions to begin to surface. It is not uncommon for people to experience a wave of emotion, a welling up of tears, while getting a massage or holding a yoga pose. Mindfulness and somatic focusing also can illicit the surfacing of suppressed emotions, and are excellent practices for learning to be with and manage our emotions.

From the yogic perspective, emotions are energy moving through the energy system of the body, especially the psychospiritual centers of consciousness, known as the chakras. Chakras represent feeling centers in the body and have been described as psychic centers in the body where energy, consciousness, and emotions come together. When we suppress emotions, the energy is put into storage. This suppressed energy creates patterns that are then held in our energy field. These patterns, with their belief systems, become part of the perceptual lens through which we see the world. We will be talking more about perceptual lenses in the next chapter.

These stored patterns and emotions become blocks to the movement of energy through the body and create blocks and imbalances in the chakras. The chakra affected depends on the type of emotion being suppressed. From this perspective, the chakras are major determinants of our health and well-being. As we recognize and allow the emotion, we can take our attention to and breathe in and out of the chakra that corresponds with the emotion we are experiencing. This is called Chakra Breathing and also helps unblock and shift the energy. **In directly experiencing our emotions, we choose to embrace what is being experienced; both the emotion and the bodily felt sensation. We open to "being with" rather than avoiding our experience**. Much has been written about the chakras; however, it too, is beyond the scope of this book. I have included some books that relate to the chakras in the Recommended Reading section.

As I've mentioned and will be discussing further in this chapter, both unconscious beliefs and emotions, directly and significantly, affect our health and well-being. I will be focusing on our conscious and unconscious beliefs, in more depth, in later chapters. This chapter will focus mostly on addressing unconscious emotions and repressed parts of our selves. The separating of our beliefs and our emotions is for the purpose of discussion only, as they are constantly affecting each other. To set the stage for further discussion, I will briefly introduce some information that applies to both our beliefs and our emotions.

If our unconscious beliefs and emotions so powerfully shape our lives, where do these beliefs and emotions come from? If someone has experienced abuse or neglect, a traumatic event, or lived in a family affected by addiction or violence, as a child or adult, it is understandable that they would have had to suppress painful emotions. But what does one have to suppress if they come from a seemingly "normal", functional, even close and loving family? Or, who may have had challenges, but no real traumas to deal with? More than you may think.

Consider some things that we know... infants and young children are totally dependent on caretakers and have many needs to be met. There are needs for food, warmth, and relief from discomfort, as well as, the needs for attention, affection, and nurturing. Along with these, there are the needs for acceptance and celebration of the child's uniqueness and specialness; loving the child for exactly who they are. Even in the best of families, with the most well intentioned parents, no parent or parents can meet all of those needs all the time. All of us had some degree of unmet need which translated into stress and emotional pain.

This actually starts even before birth. We now know that the womb experience, which is influenced by the stress level, diet and emotional state of the mother, directly affects the developing fetus. We also know that the birth experience itself creates stress, and affects and imprints the baby (thanks to the work of Stan Grof, M.D.) Then, once born, the child is functioning in a hypnogogic state for the first six years. What this means is that the child's brain is operating at delta and theta EEG frequencies, which makes them highly suggestible and programmable. Children are programmed by their observation of and experience with others in the home. This includes the tone of voices heard, language used, emotion expressed, or not, and the treatment of people observed and experienced themselves. Children are amazingly adept at picking up on the energy of people around them, even when it is not directly expressed, or acted on. In this hypnogogic state, the conclusions drawn from the above are deeply encoded as truth. It is these unconscious, core beliefs that shape and can determine our lives.

Another factor that I will mention here is that all of the above, and more, effect the development of the child's ego. Erik Erikson was one of the first to delineate the tasks of the ego that correlate with each developmental stage throughout the lifespan. How successfully the child masters each task influences the mastering of successive tasks and the development of the ego. For example, the first task of the infant is the issue of "trust versus mistrust," and has much to do with how well those needs were met, and what the infant experienced. The conclusions that are drawn form the basis of the early core beliefs. Beliefs created from the child's experience of whether or not her needs were met, she was mirrored, and she felt safe. Since the caretakers are the whole world to the infant, those experiences and beliefs get extrapolated to the world and to life, as well. I believe Einstein said something to the effect of, "One of the most important questions to be answered is: Is the universe friendly?" We answer it unconsciously at a very early age.

To this discussion of where unconscious beliefs and emotions come from, one more piece of the puzzle is worth considering. An aspect of yogic philosophy that was further delineated by Carl Jung also addresses our emotions and our unconscious. The yogis believe that the material world manifests as pairs of opposites, and say, "The one thing always comes as two." Our minds then split the world and we make a judgment, choosing one side and rejecting the other. This is dualistic thinking that leads to an either/or frame of reference. We choose and feel attached to what is acceptable and we reject and feel aversion towards what is not acceptable. We do this with everything, including parts of ourselves and our emotions. We split the world into what's "me" and what's "not me", which we repress (Jung's shadow). Sometimes we don't know what we're feeling because the emotion is judged as unacceptable and therefore repressed.

Both emotions and parts of our selves get repressed if they go against what got us attention or approval. The parts of us that got us attention or approval became how we presented ourselves to the world and believed ourselves to be (Jung's persona). Basically, the aspects of our selves that got approval were the ones that got developed and became parts of our conscious personality or persona.

The polar opposites of those aspects became parts of our shadow, which we deny, but which remain residents of our unconscious, who sooner or later have their say, and who sometimes get acted out unconsciously, often to our total embarrassment. What we deny, we also project onto others. We repress many parts of ourselves, especially those that were not approved of in our families, social groups, or culture. We all have many sub-personalities, or what Brugh Joy, M.D. called our "community of selves" that reside in our unconscious and have a major influence on our lives.

That is why part of our transformation is to increasingly let go of an exclusive identification with our persona. This is another way of saying what I referred to in Chapter One as dis-identifying with our egos to open to a larger sense of our selves. The self-healing capacity of the psyche seeks to unite and synthesize. This self-healing drive seeks to integrate everything split off from consciousness by fear and suppression. Its goal is to bring unconscious material to conscious awareness, so it can be integrated into the personality, and the individual can become more authentic and whole. This is Jung's process of individuation. The yogis taught that the polarities are inseparable, so that when you banish part, you diminish yourself. Ramakrishna said, "This whole world is God alone. I raise both my hands to it all. It is all life, it is all God." For yogis, it is in meditation, when the body and mind are quieted, that emotions and banished parts of ourselves begin to surface.

Jung's concept of the shadow represents these repressed parts of our selves, along with their related beliefs and emotions. We are not aware of them consciously, but they come out as symptoms, patterns in our lives, and in dreams. What we're often not aware of is that our unconscious tends to have a greater influence in our lives than anything we are consciously aware of. Relationships are significantly affected by this as we project our disowned feelings and qualities onto other people. **Qualities in others that we find attractive or admirable, as well as, repulsive and aversive, are actually unacknowledged or unaccepted qualities in ourselves that we have repressed and then projected onto them.**

Reclaiming our shadow projections, both dark and light, is another way that we become more whole and make our egos healthier. The work is to make what is unconscious, conscious, and to integrate the polarities into our conscious personalities, thereby becoming whole human beings. Jung was quoted as saying, "Whatever aspect you repress will come back to you as an intruder, as fate." So, like the yogis, bring it all up into the light of awareness and be willing to be with it consciously.

Journaling and working with our dreams are two highly effective practices for doing this. Journaling honest, uncensored thoughts and feelings, grease the pump, so to speak, and pave the way for unacknowledged thoughts and feelings to begin to present themselves to our conscious awareness. Journaling is one of the first practices I recommend to clients because it is a powerful therapeutic agent.

EXERCISE

> As part of your daily quiet time, write down your honest, uncensored thoughts and feelings. This gives acknowledgement and expression to your emotions which allows the energy to shift, and often brings clarity and new insight into yourself and your life.
>
> It is helpful to not judge your emotions as good or bad, right or wrong. Emotions are just part of what it means to be human and how we are designed to express our experience of life. What we do with the emotions, in terms of our behaviors, certainly can be constructive or destructive, but the emotions themselves are not.
>
> Some of your emotions may not feel comfortable, but if you can bear the discomfort, they will move through you and be a source of healing and liberation.

Journaling provides a container that can hold what you are feeling. The journal needs to be confidential and kept in a safe, private place, so that you can be as open and honest as possible. It is where you get to speak your truth – "the good, the bad and the ugly." Julia Cameron, in her book, *The Artist's Way* presents the practice of doing "morning pages" each morning as a way to unleash your creativity, get to know yourself, and tap into your purpose and passion.

Long suppressed, or overwhelming emotions, often feel too dangerous to acknowledge or feel. This is when counseling with a trained therapist is of tremendous value. The therapist can safely guide and support you through the emotional terrain and provide invaluable insight throughout the process. The therapeutic relationship creates a safe container for your work, and the therapist is an objective, compassionate witness to your experiences, which, is very healing and transformative.

Working with your dreams allows you direct access to your unconscious material. Dreams seek to inform you about what you are not aware of consciously and reveal your shadow elements. This work aids you in owning your polarities and the dark, unacceptable parts of yourself. You keep learning to accept, own and acknowledge "I am that, too." Dreams also show you your highest self, your true potential, and your innate goodness and beauty.

As Jeremy Taylor, author of several books on dreams, has said, "Dreams always come in the service of healing and wholeness." Dream analysis is a primary part of Jungian therapy, and is an important modality for working with the dynamics of the unconscious. While having a trained analyst or therapist is tremendously helpful at times, you can become skillful at working with your dreams. Here again, there are many excellent books on dreams and dream interpretation, and a few are listed in the Recommended Reading section.

If seeing your dreams as a healing and transformative practice is new to you, I will share some introductory thoughts on dream work. The first step in dream work is the ability to remember your dreams upon awakening. Taking B 6 vitamins is believed to help with dream retention. The following suggestions can also be helpful.

Before going to sleep do the following:

1. Place a pen and paper, or tape recorder, on the nightstand for easy access.
2. Set a conscious intention to remember your dreams.
3. Tell your unconscious mind you want its wisdom and ask for its help.

Upon awakening, write down the dream to the best of your ability, even if you only remember little bits and pieces of it. Giving it a name can help with remembering it. The following practice is a way to work with the dream material.

EXERCISE

> Always notice the opening scene, if possible. It often reveals the dominant theme of the dream. Then pose questions to yourself about the dream, such as: Why did this dream come to me? And, as Jung asked, why... this dream... now?
>
> Does the dream come to compensate for something that is lacking in my conscious life?
> Does it show me an unpleasant side of myself I have avoided?
> Does it affirm me by showing me something positive in me that I have not acknowledged?
>
> Then, you can free associate with the dream by asking: What associations do I make with the people, places and events in the dream? What comes to mind as I think about the dream? Allow yourself to sense the feel-quality of the dream and ask: What did I feel in the dream and in the wake of the dream? What does this feel-quality remind me of? When did I ever feel like that? What in my life now feels like that?
>
> You can also visualize and sense the lay-out of the main place in your dream, then ask: What does it remind me of? Where have I been in a place like that? What place felt like that?
>
> It is helpful to summarize the story or plot of the dream and ask: What in my life is like that story? What theme in my life does the story reflect?
>
> Finally, notice the characters in the dream. According to some theories, all of the people in the dream are parts of the dreamer. Explore and ask: What feel-quality does this person give me? What adjective would I use for this person? Now think of that adjective or feel-quality as part of you and ask: If that is part of me, what part would that be? Also ask: How do the people in the dream get along and treat each other? How do the males and females get along and treat each other?
>
> See if an over-all theme of the dream comes to you and journal your responses.

Exploring your dreams can be fascinating and rewarding, even though at times disturbing. If dream work is not for you, there are other similar ways of accessing and working with unconscious material. These involve paying attention to your daydreams and/or fantasies, your yearnings and longings, the myths or stories that resonate with you, such as your favorite childhood fairytale, and the synchronicities that show up in your life. All of these could be considered ways in which your unconscious is trying to inform your conscious mind to offer the guidance of your innate healing wisdom.

There is one more thing I must say about dreams and working with our shadow elements, especially since this book is about transforming ourselves so that we can then be agents of transformation in our world. As I mentioned earlier, what we reject as "not me," gets suppressed and becomes our shadow, which, is then automatically and unconsciously projected onto other people and our external world (me versus you). Projection is not only an individual phenomenon, but a collective one, as well (us versus them). Groups of people, nations, and religions project their collective shadows onto other people, nations and religions. We have only to look at the "holy wars," the extermination of Jews in Nazi Germany, and in this country, the slavery of Afro-Americans, and the disenfranchisement of Native Americans, to see how a collective shadow projected onto another group then becomes the justification for hatred, injustice, and even genocide.

Projection is the root cause of all prejudice and bigotry, and is a major factor in violence and war. If we want to create a more peaceful and just world, we must reveal and own our collective shadows. That will only happen when a critical mass of individuals own their own shadows, and begin to see the other as part of themselves, and thereby, see us all as one human family.

In terms of what some of the new science is telling us, a common theme is the role of consciousness in disease and in healing. What the research is showing is that our thoughts, beliefs, and emotions play a significant role in creating our biology, and therefore, have a profound effect on our health. We are back to the concept that consciousness creates the body. Conventional medicine has acknowledged that consciousness has a significant impact on our biochemistry, as is evidenced by the initiation of the double-blind placebo testing of drugs that began in the 1950's. Pharmaceutical drugs had to prove their effectiveness when compared to sugar pills, or more precisely, the effects of the patient's belief. There have been many more recent research studies on the placebo effect.

Dawson Church, in *The Genie in your Genes*, sites specific studies involving the placebo effect. In one of the sited studies, which was published in the *New England Journal of Medicine* in 2002, Bruce Mosely, M.D., an orthopedic surgeon at Baylor University Medical Center, wanted to find out which of two surgical procedures produced the best cure rate for osteoarthritic knees. Church describes the study which I will summarize. The two surgical procedures were debridement and lavage. Patients needing the surgery were divided into two groups, one receiving debridement and the other lavage. To control for the placebo effect, Dr. Mosely instituted a third group. This group received neither debridement nor lavage. This group was taken into surgery, but only given the incision that would indicate that the surgery had been performed and sown back up. No surgery was done on their knees.

Post-operative results were compared for all three groups during various stages of the recovery process. They found that the placebo group's recovery rates, freedom from former pain and return of functioning of the knees was not significantly different from those of the surgical groups. The patients' beliefs that it would be beneficial were as effective as the actual procedure. Dr. Moseley and his staff were astounded. This demonstrates our bodies' self-healing capacities, and validates what we refer to as "mind over matter".

It has become well accepted that stress is a major factor in disease. And stress comes down to unresolved emotions. A 2004, University of Kentucky, 30-year meta-analysis study on psychological stress and the immune system found that 85% of illness is the result of chronic stress (SC Segerstrom and GE Miller). I have seen even higher percentages. John Sarno, M.D., an orthopedist, wrote the book, *The Mindbody Prescription,* and based his practice on evidence he found that despite what the x-rays may show, some forms of chronic pain were, at root, the mindbody's way of distracting the person from unresolved, unconscious emotions.

In subsequent chapters we will be looking at some of the new research that has come out of the fields of cellular biology and neurocardiology which also validates the role of our beliefs and emotions in creating disease or in creating optimal health and well-being. There is no question that addressing unresolved emotion, both conscious and unconscious, is a key factor in healing, well-being and transformation.

As we allow emotions to surface, be acknowledged and experienced, we find that both pleasant and unpleasant emotions move through us fairly quickly. We can then fully experience the feeling without acting on it until we decide the most appropriate action. As Stephen Cope says, "What if there was no feeling that was not workable? That would be freedom! All feelings would be OK. We could face anything". Journaling and working with dreams or other aspects of our inner world facilitate the surfacing of unconscious material so it can be acknowledged and released.

Practicing witness consciousness or mindfulness as discussed in Chapter One and somatic focusing, as discussed in Chapter Two, enable us to be with the emotions that surface and observe and experience them without being overwhelmed by them. Remember, this witness consciousness is our Higher Self and our inner companion and friend. Cope also says, "We can bear anything if we have company – a companion". **As we face difficult emotions, we now have a best friend to be with us. It is our Self, offering that interior gesture of friendship to our smaller self/ego. This Self-self relationship is of utmost importance and is where we can "reparent" ourselves**.

Hopefully I have made a case for the necessity of addressing your emotions and your unconscious mind in this transformational process. In review, how do you access unconscious beliefs and emotions? You begin by no longer resisting them and by being willing to tolerate discomfort and face some of your fears. Secondly, you need to stop the constant busyness and doing, and be willing to spend some time in silence, with yourself, just being. What I refer to as a daily quiet time. Then, you can engage in one of the various forms of bodywork, begin using some of the practices I have presented and for additional help consider seeking some counseling.

The overriding point related to your emotions and your unconscious that I want you to take with you is the shift from avoiding to embracing, which entails the willingness to "be with" and embrace, rather than, resist and avoid any emotion or aspect of yourself. The sacred attention I mentioned in Chapter One is invaluable here for it enables you to behold whatever aspect of yourself has come up with reverence and appreciation, knowing it is in the service of wholeness.

You take all of yourself and your feelings into your own heart with compassion and acceptance. This means you stop seeing the uncomfortable aspects of your experience as something to get rid of, rather than welcoming them and seeing them as gifts, as agents of healing and transformation. In opening to your unconscious, you are accessing a larger consciousness. One in which you move beyond dualism and the either/or mentality to embrace a both/and frame of reference. As the renowned mythologist Joseph Campbell suggests, "You say yeah to it all" and you learn to hold the tension of opposites so they can be integrated and you can become more **whole.**

Chapter Four: Reacting to Choosing
The Perceptual Lens through Which We See the World and Create Our Reality

In the last chapter, we explored the importance of working with our emotions and our unconscious mind. We looked at how core beliefs and related emotions get established, and how we can work with this unconscious terrain for healing and transformation. I introduced the concept that emotions are energy designed to move through us, and for that reason, emotions need to be acknowledged, accepted and released. From an energetic perspective, emotions that are suppressed "freeze" the energy, which is then stored in our energy field, creating blocks to the movement of energy and to our health and well-being.

However, emotions are not just energy; they are actually energy + information. This information consists of the beliefs that relate to the emotion and which we hold in our energy field as patterns of related beliefs. Knowing this, we can think of our emotions as energy + beliefs. In this chapter, we will explore how these emotions and beliefs create our reality, and how we can shift from emotional reactivity to emotional self-management. This allows us to choose how we respond to life, and to create the life that we desire.

Gary Kraftsow, founder of the Viniyoga Institute, and author of *Yoga for Wellness*, states that to work with an emotion, one has to change the energetic and release the storyline. In other words, to work with our emotions, we first move and balance the energy which then changes the physiology. Releasing the storyline involves releasing the belief and related stories we have told ourselves, related to the belief. To do this, it's helpful to understand a little more about the physiology involved and about the stories we hold in consciousness. These stories are based, in large measure, on those core beliefs that were established early on and then are reinforced throughout our lives. The aspect of our physiology that I will focus on in this chapter is the autonomic nervous system.

Our sensory organs and heart are constantly reading the environment and inputting informational signals into the system. Our ancient survival mechanisms scan the input looking for threats to our survival so that if threatened, we can fight, flee, or freeze. This is what we now call the stress response. This instinctual response involves the limbic brain and the autonomic nervous system. The autonomic nervous system is comprised of two sub-systems. They are the sympathetic nervous system, which initiates the stress response, and the parasympathetic system, which initiates the relaxation and healing response. When the stress response is initiated, chemicals and hormones are released into the body. As a result, the heart rate, blood sugar level and blood pressure increase; blood drains from the head and core to peripheral muscles for action; breathing becomes fast and shallow; and muscles tense.

In this process, the functioning of higher reasoning, along with the functioning of the immune, digestive, eliminative, and reproductive systems are shut down. Ultimately, this stress response is experienced as emotion (fear, anxiety, anger, guilt, overwhelm, sadness). The stress response, while necessary for survival, puts the system in the defense mode and is a major drain on the mindbody.

The parasympathetic system is designed to turn on when the stress is over, so the system can repair the damage done during the stress. It shifts the system into the self-healing and growth mode. Chronic stress inhibits the functioning of every system in the body, creates a feedback loop of negative emotions, and keeps the parasympathetic system turned off, which disables the body's self-healing mechanisms. For mental and emotional well-being and optimal health we need a balanced autonomic nervous system - one in which the sympathetic and parasympathetic systems balance each other. A certain amount of stress is good as long as it is intermittent and interspersed with parasympathetic activation.

To have a sense of how the autonomic nervous system works, we have to know a little more about the nature of the brain. It is the limbic brain's thalamus that receives signals from the senses and the heart, and that sends signals to other parts of the brain and to the autonomic nervous system. To simplify, in the evolution of our brain and consciousness we developed multiple brains. The brain stem, which surrounds the top of the spinal cord, is the most primitive part of the brain. It regulates basic life functions like breathing, and is referred to as the reptilian brain. The limbic system surrounds the brain stem and added emotional components to the brain's capacities. It also coordinates the activity of higher and lower brain structures. In addition to the thalamus, another part of the limbic system is the amygdala.

The amygdala stores and processes emotional memories – all of the wounds, hurts, traumas, and fears one has experienced, so that when new situations arise that have a similar emotional tone, the threat is recognized and we can react. The amygdala signals the sympathetic nervous system, which then initiates the stress response. Like the reptilian brain, it is basically defensive and survival oriented. Incoming information is accessed for threat potential based on the stored significance from the past, often from childhood or times when we were dependent and vulnerable. The current situation may not be the same as the stored past experience, it just has to have a similar emotional feel or tone. If it does, the stress response is automatically triggered. With this response we're limited to a defensive reaction.

In its evolution the brain then developed the neocortex, the most evolved part of the brain. This gave us the ability to think and speak, and then process incoming information by accessing higher reasoning, logical analysis, and creativity. In the cortex are the prefrontal lobes. Among other functions, the prefrontal lobes regulate emotion and emotionally-attuned communications. They are involved in what is called "response flexibility," which is the ability to take in information, think about it, consider options, and produce an adaptive response. Now, incoming information can be assessed from a much larger perspective where we have a **choice** as to how we want to respond; then it goes to the amygdala, where, if there actually is a threat, the stress response can be activated. This part of the brain, especially the pre-frontal lobes, was designed to be linked to the "heart brain," which we'll be addressing in a later chapter.

Unfortunately, despite having a neocortex, we often get stuck in old patterning, or have the stored past experience too easily triggered. Once the stress response is initiated, the higher cortical functioning is shut down, along with its objectivity, reasoning capabilities, and creativity. Doc Childre and Deborah Rozman, Ph.D., of the Institute of HeartMath, in their book, *Transforming Depression* state, "The part of the brain that gets activated under stress stays active long after the stressful situations are over, which may explain why it's hard for many people to let stressful feelings go." They continue, "If your body experiences a particular emotional state repeatedly, the neural circuits for that state are reinforced, which means you've literally built in a physical pathway that makes it easier to feel those stressful emotions."

We know this to be true based on Hebb's axiom which states that neuronets that fire together wire together. (In 1949 Donald Hebb, a neurological researcher, discovered that neurons in the brain that "fire" at the same time become linked). The more stress we've had, the more neuronets are firing and pathways being etched into the limbic area of the brain. If there is more neural circuitry between the thalamus and the amygdala than there is between the thalamus and the frontal cortex, more signals are likely to go right to the amygdala.

Over time, incoming input more easily goes directly to the amygdala, rather than the frontal cortex, and that becomes our default mode for responding to life, reflected in a pattern of emotional reactivity. We tend to keep the sympathetic nervous system turned on and we experience more anger, fear, anxiety, and sadness. It becomes a negative feedback loop: negative outlook, negative feelings, negative experiences, and more neuronets. As you can see, there are two tracks in the brain which incoming information can take. They are the short track of thalamus directly to amygdala (threat/react), or the long track of thalamus to pre-frontal cortex (reason/choice) and then to amygdala.

Childre and Rozeman also reference recent research by Dr. Helen Mayberg that identified an area of the brain, called area 25, that is "a key conduit of neural traffic between the brain's thinking centers (in the frontal cortex) and emotional and memory centers (in the limbic system)... The current theory is that Area 25 is part of a neural and hormonal survival system to respond to acute threats, but this system turns corrosive when stress memories and persistent negative thoughts trigger the survival system continuously... Area 25 is like a switch in the circuit. If you can trip the circuit out of survival mode, then the body and brain can settle back to normal."

The Institute for HeartMath has developed techniques to facilitate that switch. A significant part of this switch is the balancing of the autonomic nervous system, which is done through practices that promote self-regulation, such as the ones you've been practicing in each chapter. In this chapter, I will share practices and techniques that directly affect the autonomic nervous system and our energetic field where these thoughts, beliefs, and emotions are stored.

We can think of the autonomic nervous system as one aspect of the energy part of emotion. The stored significance in the amygdala, the related core beliefs, and our prevailing thoughts are the information part of emotion. This includes all those messages we received growing up from family, teachers, religion, and society - the messages that shaped our beliefs about ourselves, others, the world, and God. Remember the beliefs that I mentioned in the last chapter relating to: Is the universe friendly? Can I trust (trust vs. mistrust)? Am I safe? Am I loveable as I am? Am I enough? Is there enough? Will my needs be met? These beliefs become the perceptual lens through which we see the world and are a major determinant of our moods and emotions.

This information literally becomes a filter or lens that determines how we perceive ourselves, others, and the world. Research on the relationship between perception and belief has been done at Harvard Medical School and other major research institutions. One study was done in which kittens were raised for their first four months in an environment with only horizontal or vertical lines. They found, for example, that as adult cats those raised with only horizontal lines could not "see" vertical lines, only horizontal lines. The cats would run into the legs of chairs and tables because they could not "see" them (Leventhal and Hirsch, *Science*, 28 November 1975).

In another study, fish were put in a large fish tank with a clear divider panel in the center. The fish could see the fish on the other side of the divider, but could not swim with them. After a period of time the divider was removed, which would allow all the fish to swim around the entire tank. They found that a significant number of the fish continued to swim only in the side of the tank that they had been previously limited to. On a similar note, I heard Deepak Chopra, M.D. relate that in India they would train a baby elephant to stay where they wanted it to by tying a flimsy rope on the elephant to a stake. As an adult elephant, not even a thick iron chain attached to a large tree could keep the elephant in place, but tie a flimsy rope to a stake and the elephant would stay there indefinitely.

Chopra goes on to say that our sensory apparatus and neural circuitry develop as a result of initial sensory experiences, then reinforce what we originally experienced by limiting what we perceive to that which reinforces what we already know. He calls these assumptions "premature cognitive commitments" and goes on to say we freeze this information into a perceptual reality based on our cognitive commitments. **It has recently been verified that at any given moment, 2.3 million bits of information enter our perceptual field, but we are able to process only 132 bits!! So what is it that filters 132 bits out of a potential of 2.3 million? It's our beliefs acting as a perceptual lens that**

does the filtering. We can only perceive what we've already been preprogrammed to see, making it a rather limited and distorted view. The science is new, but the wisdom has been around for ages. The Talmud teaches, "We don't see the world as it is, we see the world as we are."

We know that our beliefs and emotions, both conscious and unconscious, create the perceptual lens through which we see the world and shape our reality. Therefore, do we want a perceptual lens based on the survival/limbic brain, defensive reactivity, and fear? Or, a lens based on the growth/frontal brain, creative choice, and love? To more and more consistently live from the perspective of the latter, we must change the energetic and the information. What tools are effective in addressing these?

To change the energetic, which involves, in part, the autonomic nervous system, the yogis are the masters, and yoga offers highly effective practices. I introduced breath awareness and diaphragmatic breathing in Chapter Two. In his book, *The Relaxation Response*, Herbert Benson, M.D. writes of his research at Harvard Medical School. They found that diaphragmatic breathing, progressive muscle relaxation, and a meditative focus turned off the stress response (sympathetic nervous system) and turned on the relaxation response (parasympathetic nervous system). Long term practice of meditation, which we will discuss in the next chapter, has been correlated with greater control of the autonomic nervous system.

Yogis have demonstrated to Western scientists at the Menninger Clinic their ability to voluntarily control bodily processes such as heart activity, skin temperature, and blood flow, normally considered to beyond voluntary control. Yoga teaches many breath practices that balance the autonomic nervous system through regulating the rhythm of the inhalation and exhalation. One of the pranayamas, or breath practices, is alternate nostril breathing. This practice, in particular, is known to regulate and bring balance to the autonomic nervous system. Many yoga classes include pranayama as part of the class. Information can also be obtained on it through publications of the Himalayan Institute Press.

The breath and asanas free up and move energy through the system, helping to unblock the frozen energy resulting from the beliefs and emotions that were suppressed and stored in the energy field. Systematic relaxation teaches us how to consciously relax tense muscles and bring both the mind and the body into a state of deep relaxation, switching us into the parasympathetic nervous system. Just like when the stress response is activated and a signal is sent to muscles to tense, the reverse happens. When muscles are chronically tense, a signal is sent that indicates to the brain that there must be a threat, so the stress response stays activated, even if there is no actual stressor. As mentioned in Chapter Two, yoga classes generally end with some form of systematic relaxation, and there are wonderful guided relaxation CDs that are available.

In the next chapter, we will be exploring meditation and mindfulness, which are yogic practices that address our beliefs and the storylines they create. We will also explore cognitive therapy, which helps us to change conscious thoughts and beliefs in order to change the way we feel. In that chapter, we will be looking at some of the new science in the fields of cellular biology and epigenetics which validates the importance of addressing beliefs, and validates what the yogis have been teachings for ages. If we accept what the new sciences are telling us about the power of beliefs, then we will want to consider our thoughts and beliefs with great care.

To quote Gregg Braden, in the introduction to *The Spontaneous Healing of Belief* "Paradigm-shattering experiments published in leading-edge, peer-reviewed journals reveal that we're bathed in a field of intelligent energy that fills what used to be thought of as empty space. Additional discoveries show beyond any reasonable doubt that this field responds to us – it rearranges itself – in the presence of our heart-based feelings and beliefs. And this is the revolution that changes everything." What this means is that our beliefs and emotions matter! The universe will literally re-arrange itself to accommodate our prevailing beliefs. Our beliefs and our perceptual lens literally do create our reality. As Henry Ford said, "Whether you believe you will succeed or you will fail, you're right."

Knowing the urgency of healing beliefs and emotions, and their relationship to our energy system (beliefs are maintained by the suppressed energy patterns that are held in our field causing blocks or imbalances), we now have new resources to help us. In addition to the previously mentioned practices, we have the new field of energy psychology, which has grown out of Chinese medicine and the use of acupressure points on the meridian system for healing. Meridians are the energy pathways that run through the body in Chinese medicine. Meridian therapy proposes that all disturbed physical, mental, and emotional states correspond to specific states of meridian energy imbalance. Therefore, the most direct and efficient approach to changing our state is by addressing the energy system of the body directly. Once the meridian is balanced the belief or emotion can shift.

Stimulation of acupuncture points by tapping with our fingers, or by applying light pressure is very effective in balancing the meridian energy system. Research on the various acupressure points reveal certain ones have the ability to unblock and re-establish balance in the energy system, specifically related to beliefs and emotions. By stimulating the points through tapping, while focusing the mind on the unhealthy belief or disturbing emotion, the system has the capacity to reframe the issue, and balance the energy, thus allowing the old belief or emotion to be released. When our energy system moves toward a more balanced state, we become more resourceful and our system's ability to regulate itself is restored. New, healthier beliefs and emotions can then be installed and energetically re-enforced through the same process.

There are many different styles of meridian therapy. (See the Recommended Reading section.). Most of the approaches share two common components. The first component is to consciously focus on the issue of your concern. Having brought your issue to mind, you simply notice how this feels in your body, rather than analyzing the issue mentally. Sensing how this feels in your body, rather than analyzing the issue in your head, connects you with the field of energy that reflects your emotional experience. Having connected to your energy field, you proceed to the second common component. This involves stimulating meridian points, usually by holding or tapping, to rebalance the imbalances in the energy systems that are relative to your issue. Each approach has its unique variation on how the second component is performed.

EXERCISE

Here are the basic steps:

1. Begin by identifying the issue you want to work on (e.g. an emotion: "I'm angry at Susan" or a belief: "No matter what I do, it's not enough").
2. Similar to somatic focusing which we discussed in chapter two, you acknowledge *where* in your body you feel the discomfort that is related to your issue. Next, notice how this feeling *feels* in your body (tight, tingly, knotted, vacant). Then, observe the *intensity* of your discomfort and rate it on a scale of 1 to 10, where 10 is the most intense.
3. Place your hand on your chest at the heart area. Rub your hand in a clockwise direction over your chest, repeating the following statement *3 times*. "I deeply and completely love and accept myself even though ... (state the truth of your issue here, e.g. "I have all this anger toward Susan" or "I believe no matter what I do it's not enough").
4. Tap or hold the designated points, based on the technique you are using, while you remind yourself of and focus on your issue. A commonly used sequence is:
Inner Eyebrows
Side of Eyes
Below Eyes
Under Nose
Under Lip
Below Collar Bones
Below Armpits
At the end of the tapping sequence, take in a deep breath and let it out. Do the tapping or holding series followed by a deep breath *3 times*. Then re-evaluate your level of discomfort (scale of 1 to 10).
5. Repeat step 4 until you feel comfortable with your issue. Once this occurs, shift your attention to the positive outcome you desire related to the issue (state a more positive emotion or belief about yourself, e.g. "I'm now able to let go and experience peace" or "I am supported, resourceful and content"). While focusing on the positive outcome, perform step 4. This will help to integrate the positive experience.

Roger Callahan, Ph.D., is the originator of Thought Field Therapy (TFT) and is one of the early developers and practitioners of meridian therapy. An outgrowth of TFT is the Emotional Freedom Technique (EFT) which was developed by Gary Craig and on which the above practice is based. I prefer this technique because of its ease. Another technique that I have found to be effective is the Tapas Acupressure Technique (TAT) developed by Tapas Fleming, A.P.

The techniques and practices that I have discussed in this book so far all have a proven record of effectiveness. **We *can* reprogram our autonomic nervous system and we *can* change even old, long-standing beliefs if we are willing to incorporate the suggested practices into our lives and engage in them diligently and consistently. In learning how to self-regulate and balance our nervous system, and release and rewrite old programming, we can change the perceptual lens through which we see the world and create our reality.** By shifting from reacting to choosing, we take control of our mental and emotional states, and our lives. Then we have the opportunity to begin creating the reality that we want – better health, better relationships, greater peace, joy and love. As a yogi once said, "We forgo a fate in favor of a destiny." We are much more powerful than we ever imagined!

And as we go, so goes our world. So once again we are back to doing this work not only for ourselves, but for the collective. We won't have peace in our world until we have peace in our own heart, in our own family, neighborhood, city, and nation. Consciousness (our beliefs and emotions) not only creates the body, it creates our lives and our world. Consider this passage from Gregg Braden's *The Spontaneous Healing of Belief:*

"If we can accept the powerful evidence that consciousness itself and our role in it are the missing links in the theories of how reality works, then everything changes… It writes us – all of humankind – right back into the equation of the universe. It also casts us into the role of solving the great crises of our day, rather than leaving them to a future generation or simply to fate. As we are architects of our reality, with the power to rearrange the atoms of matter itself, what problem cannot be solved and what solution could possibly be beyond our reach?"

Chapter Five: Past/Future to Present Moment
The Primacy of the Mind and the Present Moment in Transformation

We ended Chapter Four addressing the power of our beliefs and emotions in shaping our reality, and the new field of Energy Psychology with its techniques for changing disturbing beliefs and feelings. In this chapter, I want to start with more of the new science that also verifies the power of our beliefs and their role in our health and well-being. The practices we will be exploring to work with our mind and our emotions, also reveal the importance of learning to live in the present moment and help us to do so. Ultimately, the shift in consciousness we want to make is from living in the past or the future, to living our lives more and more in the here and now.

The following, is a brief overview of some of the new findings in the fields of cellular biology and epigenetics. Bruce Lipton, Ph.D., research scientist and former medical school professor, has turned the world of cellular biology upside down. According to Lipton, who has written the book, *The Biology of Belief*, until recently it was thought that all genes were self-activating. This meant that genes could "turn themselves on (express themselves) and off," which is why it was believed that genes control biology. He goes on to say that a radically new understanding has emerged at the leading edge of cell science. It is now recognized that the environment, and more specifically, the perception of the environment, is what directly controls the activity of our genes. Most genes, themselves, cannot self-activate. It is a signal from the environment that activates the expression of the gene.

The perception of the environment controls genes through a process known as epigenetic control. Epi, meaning above, suggests that the control comes from something above the genes. The old thinking was that the genes, in the nucleus of the cell, controlled the cell and were the command center of the cell. The behavior of the cell was programmed by the genes. The research has found that the command center is above the cell, and is actually the membrane around the cell, which reads signals from the environment and thereby activates the cell. The function of the cell membrane is perception, specifically awareness of environmental signals. It is the perception of the environment read through the signals received by the membrane that controls the cells. The behavior of the cell is not programmed, but constantly responding and adjusting to environmental signals.

At the cellular level, we literally adjust our genes to fit the environment that is perceived. At the human level, it is our beliefs that greatly influence these environmental signals. Our beliefs can influence our genes, for good or for ill. Lipton states, "This breakthrough in biology is fundamental in all healing, for it recognizes that when we change our perception or beliefs, we send totally different messages to our cells and reprogram their expression. The new biology reveals why people can have spontaneous remissions or recover from injuries deemed to be permanent disabilities." Unfortunately, the opposite is also true.

Far too often, due to our beliefs, the reprogramming is negative and leads to disease. The good news is that we can change our beliefs, and in changing our beliefs, change the signals received by the cells. How exciting is this? If you are interested, another good book on epigenetics is *The Genie in your Genes* by Dawson Church. He explores this topic in depth and discusses the on-going research in the field.

Lipton describes the genes in the cells as being programmed like software with two modes: growth (healthy functioning) or protection (impaired functioning). Does this sound familiar? When I talked about the autonomic nervous system and the stress response in the last chapter, I stated that when an incoming signal is perceived as a "threat", the sympathetic nervous system is activated and the stress response is initiated, putting the system into protection mode. This automatically shuts down the growth/healing mode (parasympathetic nervous system) and impairs the functioning of the immune and other systems. Our perceptual lens and the activation of the stress response are major factors in the type of signals being received by the cells. **Those core beliefs I mentioned, such as, "the world is not a safe place", "I'm not OK," "there is not enough", "I can't," along with our prevailing thoughts and attitudes, thereby determine our biology and health, as well as, our reality!**

Lipton recommends the use of Energy Psychology techniques to address old programming and current beliefs and attitudes that undermine our health and quality of life. As mentioned, these can be extremely beneficial, but not necessarily all that we need to do. They are very effective in addressing beliefs and emotions as we become aware of them, but they are not as helpful in addressing the stream of thoughts and the running commentary that are constantly, minute by minute, running the show, often just below the surface of our awareness. We need to have a way to become aware of these thoughts that are running 24/7, and we need to have a way to manage and change these thoughts as well.

Learning how to monitor our thoughts is an essential skill if we want to be able to manage our thoughts and emotions. This is where cognitive therapy can be helpful. Albert Ellis, M.D., a Manhattan psychiatrist, is a forerunner in the field of cognitive therapy. He claimed to have been inspired by the quote from Epictetus in the 1st century AD, which said, "People are disturbed not by things, but by the views which they take of them." Ellis developed Rational Emotive Therapy and taught his patients what he called the "ABCs."

He taught that we are all brought up to believe that there is an Activating Event (A), something happens, someone says or does something, and we have an Emotional Consequence (C), we feel happy, sad, angry, guilty. We look to the event (person, place, situation) and hold it responsible for our emotional reaction (how we feel). A causes C, so to speak. We learn this through a multitude of experiences: we brought home good grades and that made dad happy; we lied to our mother and that made her angry. So when our brother broke our favorite toy, we blamed him for making us sad, and on and on. The problem with this thinking is that it creates what Ellis called "emotional victimhood." What he meant by that was, that if that is true, then we can only feel good and be happy if everyone does what we want them to do and treats us the way we want to be treated; we always do what we think we should; and life basically goes the way we want it to, or think it should. If those things don't happen, then we are left feeling angry, sad, hurt. Since we cannot change or control other people and life, and they are responsible for how we feel, that leaves us powerless over our emotions. Therein, lies the emotional victimhood.

Fortunately, that is not the way it works. There is an intervening principle, the B, which stands for Belief. In reality, it is not the activating event that determines how we feel; it is what we tell ourselves about the event (our belief) that determines how we feel. It is not A that causes C, but the Belief about A that causes C. What this means is that we are responsible for how we feel and that we cannot really blame events for our feelings. Initially, we may not be thrilled with the concept, but it is very good news because it frees us from emotional victimhood. We may not be able to control or change other people or life, but we can learn to change our beliefs about other people, ourselves, and life and thereby change the way we feel. This changes our perceptual lens and our reality.

We have the power within us to take charge of our emotions by weeding out the self-talk/beliefs that produce disturbing feelings and substitute beliefs that produce positive feelings. Ellis was big on challenging all "should" and "must" beliefs; he called them irrational thoughts. He also stressed the importance of not "awfulizing" or "catastrophising" over events. He would suggest that patients instead tell themselves that "nothing is awful; it's only a pain in the ass." If we recall the stored significance in the amygdala, Ellis is suggesting that, as the HeartMath people say, we "take the significance out" of the situation by changing our beliefs about it.

By seeing the connection between our thoughts and our emotions, we can choose to consciously pay more attention to our thoughts, and when we are upset, look for what we were saying to ourselves just prior to feeling upset. As we recognize and change the beliefs, over time, we have the potential to change our response to people, places, and things. For more information on cognitive therapy see the Recommended Reading section.

Cognitive therapy teaches us a way to work with our mind and our thoughts on a more moment to moment basis. However, what makes cognitive therapy work is that it utilizes the frontal cortex with its logic and reasoning capacities, but if we are programmed to go right to the amygdala and react, the frontal cortex is shut down and we're stuck in the old programming. Cognitive therapy is much more effective when it is combined with the practice of mindfulness which I introduced in Chapter One and will discuss further, later in this chapter. Several of the newest forms of therapy are mindfulness-based cognitive therapies. Acceptance and Commitment Therapy (ACT) and Dialectical Behavior Therapy (DBT) both incorporate mindfulness training into the treatment process. The reason this makes the therapy more effective is that mindfulness is a skill that enables us to alter the track of incoming signals so they don't go right to the amygdala. Then the signals can be routed to the frontal cortex where we can use the cognitive therapy and choose to substitute new, healthier beliefs and/or use the skill of mindfulness to observe our thoughts with non-judgmental awareness, dis-identify with them, and let them go.

This idea of the power of the mind as both a potential asset and a major liability to our health and well-being is nothing new. The Yogis have been teaching this for thousands of years and codified the teachings in the Yoga Sutras. Sutra is the Sanskrit word for thread (of thought). The first 4 sutras of the first padas (chapter) translated from Sanskrit go as follows:

1. The mind alone is the cause of man's bondage and man's liberation.
2. Yoga is the mastery of the modifications or waves of the mind.
3. Then the seer abides in its own nature (pure consciousness knows itself).
4. At other times (the seer) is identified with the modifications of the mind. (Consequently, we become identified with our thoughts and emotions.)

That is why one aspect of mindfulness is the practice of attending to your moment to moment sensory experience. This is done by *recognizing* your thoughts, emotions, or bodily-felt sensations as they arise, then *accepting* them through non-judgmental awareness, and finally, *dis-identifying* with them. This is one of many teachings that support achieving mastery of the mind.

Mindfulness is another area that is far beyond the scope of this book, however, we have touched on these concepts in previous chapters, and we'll explore a simple mindfulness practice shortly.

The work of yoga is to remove these obstacles created by the mind. This is primarily done through the practice of meditation. There are many forms of meditation that can be practiced. In general, meditation has two important components: concentration and mindfulness. Concentration is the ability to focus the attention and sustain it. Mindfulness, as stated, is the ability to observe the workings of the mind with non-judgmental acceptance and compassion.

These two components work together to create a clear, calm, and awake mind. As the mind is cleared and calmed, we then can begin to "master the mind." So let's look at the process of moving into meditation from the yogic perspective as taught in the Himalayan Institute tradition and explained in *Yoga, Mastering the Basics*. The following are five steps:

EXERCISE

Step 1: Steady and Still. Find a proper and comfortable sitting posture such as Sukhasana, the Easy Pose, or a comfortable position where the spine is erect and arms and legs are uncrossed. Find a position where the body can remain steady and still as this helps to "steady and still" the mind. Begin relaxed breath awareness by noticing the outbreath and inbreath; be aware of the outbreath cleansing and the inbreath nourishing.

Step 2: Diaphragmatic Breathing (in seated position). Deepen the breathing and notice on the inhalation the lower abdomen expanding, and then the rib cage widening while the chest remains still. On the exhalation the abdomen falls and the rib cage narrows. Further shape the breath so that it is deep, smooth, even, and without pause or sound.

Step 3: Systematic Relaxation. Go inward and use your mind's eye to scan your body, working your way from your head to your toes relaxing and releasing any tightness or tension. Use auto-suggestion to relax or bring your awareness and the breath to each place in the body as you move from head to toes.

These three steps address the process of relaxation which prepares you for meditation. The final two steps address the process of meditation itself.

Step 4: Sustained Breath Awareness in the Nostrils. Focus your awareness on the touch of the breath at the opening of the nostrils. Notice that the outbreath is warm and the inbreath is cool. Focusing your gaze on the tip of your nose can be helpful in focusing and sustaining attention which develops concentration.

Step 5: Introduce a Mantra. In Yoga, mantras are ancient, sacred Sanskrit words that carry the vibration of sacred intention. The effect of the sound vibration helps to quiet and focus the mind. A beginning mantra that can be used is *so ham* pronounced SO HUM. It is the sound closest to the natural sound of the breath, and its Sanskrit translation is "I am That" (my inner Self is united with universal consciousness).

In this step, begin to merge the mantra with the touch of the breath in the nostrils, inhaling SO and exhaling HUM. Gradually move awareness from the breath and center your awareness in the sound where it arises in the mind. Then rest in the mantra and in the center of your being. Keep repeating the mantra and when you realize your mind has wandered, return your concentration to the mantra and resume repetition of it.

Many traditions recommend meditating for twenty minutes twice a day. Do what works for you, even if its ten minutes a day to start, and shoot for doing it five days a week. In terms of the mantra, any word or phrase can be used that is uplifting and meaningful to you. It can be simply "I am" on the inhale and "at peace" on the exhale. Mantra in Sanskrit means "protector of the mind", and in the yogic tradition is the tool for transforming the mind.

Mantras are sound vibrations that carry meaning, or said another way, they carry energy and information. Mantras are energy (breath and sound) and information (meaning). If you remember, emotion is energy and information, so we work with both to shift our emotions. Mantra repetition serves the same purpose. The breath and the sound vibration move energy and the positive meaning of the mantra is the new information   Mantras are also believed to activate a potential that lies dormant within us.

In addition to mantra repetition meditation, there is another meditative tradition that also values concentration, but goes beyond it and adds the dimension of awareness. This is mindfulness meditation, or vipassana, which was fully developed and utilized in the Buddhist tradition. We have just skimmed the surface of this ancient and codified system of training the mind.

I want to say a little more about it now and also refer you to the Recommended Reading for additional resources. Shelly Long, M.A., a mindfulness based psychotherapist, describes mindfulness as "extraordinary attentiveness to and radical acceptance of one's internal sensory experience." In particular, we focus on mental images, internal mental dialogue or self talk, body sensations, and emotions.

The mindfulness tradition teaches that much of our suffering is caused by our desire to hold on to pleasure and to resist pain. We crave and become attached to what is pleasurable and resist and feel aversion towards what is uncomfortable or painful. The problem is, in this world, pleasure doesn't last and we can't avoid pain. It is the reality of nature and of life as we know it. Our resistance to accepting this causes our suffering. I once heard it said that the equation for suffering is:

The reality of the moment x one's resistance to it = the degree of one's suffering.

The judging of our experience and our reaction to it leads to endless emotional distress. That is why cultivating acceptance of our thoughts, emotions, and the conditions of our lives is so therapeutic. In the practice, we learn to open to discomfort and detach from what we cling to. This is cultivated through experiencing the impermanence of all our thoughts, emotions and body sensations, which extrapolates to all of our experiences.

One way of practicing mindfulness meditation, which I introduced in Chapter One, is as follows:

EXERCISE

> Sit quietly, turn inward, and focus your attention on your breath. Notice your breath as it flows out and flows in... out and in. Keep your attention on your breath.
>
> As thoughts, emotions, or sensory experiences arise and your attention is drawn to them, simply be open to what arises and label the thought, emotion or sensation (such as "critical thought", "anger", "achy hip").
>
> Simply observe what your attention was drawn to without judging it, identifying with it, or creating a storyline about it. Having acknowledged, labeled, and accepted it, then let it go and gently return your attention to the breath.

The observing and labeling of your thoughts and emotions allows you to dis-identify with them making them much more manageable. The labeling has also been shown to activate the pre-frontal cortex. William Sieber, Ph.D., of the University of California, San Diego, writes, "Research has provided greater detail on how our thoughts affect bodily functions and vise versa. The body of work specifying the critical role that our frontal lobe functioning has on our emotions, and subsequently, on our physical health, has demonstrated the importance of developing greater control over the activity located in our frontal lobes (i.e. emotional and executive functioning). Such control skills will allow us to achieve optimal emotional and physical health despite stressful circumstances."

In a 2007 study done at UCLA by Matthew Lieberman, Ph.D., brain scans (fMRI) showed that when participants used labeling to name their negative emotions, the pre-frontal cortex was activated, and the amygdala was calmed. Lieberman reported that putting negative emotions into words, calms the brain's emotion center, and develops the use of a different part of the brain; literally changing the brain. We can see how this practice helps us pay attention to our present emotions, without reacting strongly to them, and it changes neural circuitry.

David Creswell, Ph.D., who was also involved in the study stated, "These findings may help explain the beneficial health effects of mindfulness meditation, and suggest an underlying reason why mindfulness meditation programs improve mood and health." Jon Kabat-Zinn, Ph.D., founder of the Stress Reduction Clinic at the University of Massachusetts Medical Center, is a great resource on mindfulness. His book, *Full Catastrophe Living,* is a practical guide to mindfulness meditation and healing, and describes the program at the Stress Reduction Clinic. I often recommend his other book, *Wherever You Go, There You Are*, as a mindfulness primer.

Another mindfulness practice is to focus intently on external sensory experiences. In Chapter One, I introduced present moment awareness, which involves intensely focusing on the sights around you, then the sounds around you and the bodily sensations you are feeling. This practice grounds you in the present moment and quiets the mind and emotions. This experience of being fully aware and present in the moment is what being "awake" and living consciously is all about. It requires that you be willing to be present to your life; the "full catastrophe" as Kabat-Zinn would say.

Another definition of mindfulness that I've come across is: the determination to be present amidst your life, as it is occurring, in the here and now, without judgment, reaction, or distraction. Mindfulness teaches you to increasingly live fully present in the moment. When you are fully present in the now, your consciousness opens to that larger, spacious awareness that is your "Self", and from which you are much more resourceful and creative.

Richard Moss, in his book, *The Mandala of Being*, talks about where the mind goes when it leaves the now. He says it goes to one of four places: me thoughts, you thoughts, thoughts about the past or thoughts about the future. Through our childhood and life experiences, the stories we create related to our core beliefs, tend to fall into these same categories. Moss suggests that we establish ME stories, YOU stories, stories that relate to the PAST, and stories that relate to the FUTURE. He encourages readers to explore and journal about the storylines they may have created, related to each of those four areas, and how they might influence their views of self, others, and life in general. This helps us identify the storylines that don't support our health and well-being.

In general, we know that focusing on the future is the cause of much of our anxieties and fears (all the "what ifs"); focusing on the past can cause feelings of regret, guilt, shame, and blame; focusing on "me" and our perceived shortcomings can cause guilt, loneliness and depression; and focusing on "you" is often the cause of resentment, anger, jealousy, and hurt. **When we are in the present moment, even if circumstances are not ideal or comfortable, we are basically OK, and are usually not in any imminent danger. We may want or need to change our circumstances, but we do not need to suffer over them. And, when we don't suffer over them, we have a clearer mind to plan what changes we need to make, and have more emotional and physical energy to initiate the desired changes.**

As we shift our consciousness to the present moment, we step out of the past, and the future, as well as, the "me," and the "you". From the now, we can let go of the old storylines, and in the present moment, clear the slate and choose to rewrite any belief that does not serve, substituting a new belief in its place. We use the Self-self relationship, and sacred attention (Chapter One), in which, we use the gaze we turn toward ourselves, to create our sense of self. As Moss says, "We can always start anew from the NOW, and create new stories".

The goal is to access and live our lives, in the present moment. This is one of the most important skills in creating and maintaining sanity and well-being in our lives. Eckert Tolle's books, *The Power of Now* and *The New Earth,* are great resources for this. Tolle encourages us to ask: "What *is* my relationship with the present moment? Do I want the present moment to be my friend or my enemy? What *is* my relationship with Life?" His message is to welcome the present moment, in whatever form it takes, and choose to make the present moment your friend; for the present moment is all we ever have, and happiness can only be experienced in the present moment.

Life is always now. If we resist the present moment and what is, we are back to resistance = suffering. Mindfulness and present moment awareness are transformational practices, and ones that truly can alleviate suffering. I have personally come to believe that three of the essentials in this process of transformation are: being rooted in Essence (Self), being rooted in the present moment, and being rooted in the heart, which we will turn to next.

Chapter Six: Head to Heart
The Heart as the Key and the Heart-Brain Connection

In the previous chapter, we looked at the power of the mind and belief, and some of the new research in the fields of cellular biology and epigenetics that confirm their role in creating our biology. The chapter ended with the practice of staying in the present moment. Three essential elements of this process of healing and transformation are: being rooted in Essence, being rooted in the present moment, and being rooted in the heart. Being rooted in Essence is experiencing, and thereby, knowing our essential nature (energy, consciousness, spirit). This is what the yogis and Jung called the Self. We then live our lives informed by that knowingness. Being rooted in the present moment is the on-going practice of bringing the mind back to now. The present moment is where we can change the belief and create a new story; where we can choose to accept what is and make the present moment our friend.

This chapter will focus on being rooted in the heart. I would like to share a story that I heard Joan Borysenko, Ph.D. tell, and that has stayed with me over the years. She spoke of a friend's near death experience. This friend was a very well educated and successful woman who had achieved status and recognition in her field. During a surgery, she died on the operating table, but was resuscitated. After the experience, she told Joan that what matters in this life is not one's curriculum vitae, one's bank account, or one's status. When all is said and done, the only thing that matters is being fully present and loving in every interaction.

After recovering, she was at her local grocery store checking out one day and noticed a look on the bag boy's face. Normally, she would have been too preoccupied with her busy life to notice the facial expression, but that day she did, and as they were walking out to her car, she commented that he looked sad. In that moment, they had a heartfelt exchange that was genuine and touching. She realized that that kind of spontaneous exchange was what matters most in life. Being rooted in the heart is having the intention to be fully present to your life. It means working toward being present and loving in every action and interaction. Let's explore some of the new science that relates to this.

The fields of neurocardiology and energy cardiology tell us that the heart is not merely a mechanical pump that circulates blood through the body. The research has revealed that the heart has a brain of its own, and an intelligence that allows it to act independently of the head brain, producing its own emotions, memories and solutions. The heart can sense, feel, remember, and process information apart from the brain. Paul Pearsall, Ph.D., a psychologist and psychoneuroimmunologist, has written a book called, *The Heart's Code*. The book explains "the heart's code", which is a subtle life energy that emanates from the heart. This code, he says, is recorded and remembered in every cell of the body, and is constantly resonating within and from us. He describes the experiences of heart transplant patients who, after receiving the new heart, took on characteristics of their donor. It was confirmed through interviews with the donor's families that these changes reflected interests or preferences of the donors. Even certain personality characteristics of the donors were exhibited in the recipients.

One recipient was reported stating, "I don't know whose heart I got, but it sure is a relaxed one. I've never felt calmer, and people seem to be more relaxed around me". Another story that Pearsall relates is of a young man's experience following his transplant. He writes, "Described by his mother as a former vegetarian, and very health conscious, he said he now craves meat and fatty foods. A former lover of heavy metal music, he said he now loves fifties rock–and-roll. He reported recurrent dreams of bright lights coming straight for him. Glenda (the donor's wife) responded, almost matter-of-factly, that her husband loved meat, was a junk food addict, and had played in a Motown/rock-and-roll band while in medical school. She, too, dreams of the lights of that fateful night." This evidence suggests that sensitive heart transplant recipients recover the cellular memories of their donors transmitted through the heart.

The Institute of HeartMath has been doing heart-brain research for over 15 years. They have found that 60% of the heart is comprised of neural tissue, and that there are major neural pathways between the heart and the brain. The heart is also now considered an endocrine gland because it makes its own hormones. A significant part of the HeartMath research focused on heart-brain communication. **With each beat, the heart not only pumps blood, but also transmits neurological, hormonal, pressure, and electromagnetic information to the brain, nervous system, and throughout the body to every cell. The heart, as the major oscillator of the body, entrains all other systems and cells, and is a frequency generator that imprints the blood with information, as well as, electrically charges it**. The HeartMath research indicates that the heart generates 40 – 60% more electrical charge than the brain, and that the brain's electromagnetic field extends a few inches from the body, whereas, the heart's field has been measured 8 feet from the body.

The heart intuitively senses what is going on in the environment and signals the brain. This heart-brain sensing or awareness actually precedes mind or conscious awareness. Researchers at the Institute of Heart Math did a study in which subjects stared at a blank computer monitor screen. At intervals, images came up on the screen. One set of images was designed to calm the subjects, as measured by brain and heart responses, and the other set of images was designed to produce an emotional response. The images were generated at random by the computer. What they discovered was that the heart responded *first*, before any mental activity had shown up on the EEG, thus indicating that the heart communicates its perceptions to the brain, rather than vise versa. What was even more intriguing was that the heart responded appropriately *before* the computer had even generated the image and flashed it on the screen.

Our heart sends out a rhythmic pattern that reflects the emotions we are feeling. The HeartMath researchers studied the rhythmic patterns of the heart, what they call heart rate variability (HRV), and found that negative, stressful emotions (anger, fear, sadness) create incoherent heart rhythms. Positive, uplifting emotions (love, awe, gratitude, care) create coherent heart rhythms. Emotional information becomes encoded into this field of the heart. This field goes to every cell in the body, transmitting signals that are read by the cell membrane, and influence cell functioning. Coherent heart rhythms generate fields that instruct cells to heal and function optimally. This is one of the ways scientists now know that emotions affect our health.

The heart communicates this information to the cells of the brain, including the thalamus, amygdala, and pre-frontal cortex. Research found that as the heart rhythm changes, so does the electrical activity in the cells of the amygdala. Coherent heart rhythms entrain and calm the amygdala. Emotional information sent from the heart to the brain also affects higher brain functions, influencing our thought processes and perceptions. What this means, is that our emotions may be the strongest determinant of the perceptual lens through which we see the world. Gregg Braden summarizes these findings: "We live in a field that reflects back to us what we feel in our hearts, not what we think in our minds." The new sciences are clearly indicating that our beliefs and our emotions are critical in our health and well-being, and that the heart is a key factor.

Before getting to the ultimate significance of the heart-brain connection, let's review the theory on the evolution of the triune, or three-part, brain introduced in Chapter Four. The first brain, which is the ancient reptilian brain, promotes physical survival and defense. It controls sensory motor functions, such as, keeping the heart beating, and the lungs breathing. The second brain is the mammalian or limbic brain, the emotional brain, which also serves the function of survival and defense. It controls emotions and memory, and is comprised of the thalamus, the amygdala, and the hippocampus. The thalamus takes incoming information from the senses and heart and sends it to the appropriate brain centers. The amygdala processes incoming information from the thalamus and stores in memory information that is threatening or emotionally significant for future reference. The hippocampus structures these memories in time.

The third brain includes the neo-cortex, which serves the function of language and thinking, along with the pre-frontal cortex, which is the executive brain and serves the functions of higher reasoning, objective analysis, and emotional communication. The pre-frontal cortex has been considered the fourth brain by some, as it represents a significant leap in consciousness. In his book, *The Death of Religion and the Rebirth of Spirit*, Joseph Chilton Pearce asserts that the prefrontal cortex is the result of evolution employing markedly different forces, what he calls "higher agencies," to bring about a far more advanced human species. He believes that these "higher agencies" translate as love of both self and other (love and altruism), and that these higher forces are both our true nature (Self), and the substantive foundation of our genetic system.

Major neural structures connect the four brains, and neural connections to the heart are part of the network. For survival purposes, the neural connections from the amygdala to the neo-cortex are stronger and more plentiful than the wiring that travels in the other direction. In our evolutionary process, the leap in consciousness achieved in the pre-frontal cortex, with its advanced intelligence and reasoning, was designed to be the major and primary pathway through which we perceive and respond to life. The neural pathways to the pre-frontal would then be the stronger, more powerful connections, and the heart-pre-frontal connection would run the show.

However, according to Pearce, those connecting loops linking the emotional-cognitive (limbic-neo-cortex) systems to the pre-frontals can be re-routed, linking the emotional-cognitive systems to the defense-survival (reptilian) system. This creates stronger and more powerful connections between the emotional-cognitive and the defensive-survival (reptilian) brain. In this case, our new brain is continually being overruled by the instinctual drives and reactivity of the old brains. Pearce believes this is a devolutionary process. He states, "An individual mind has been evolution's intent all along (as is Jung's process of individuation), however,… it gets caught up time and again in that strange tug of war between the heart-pre-frontal movement (higher evolution) and the amygdala-old brain survival reflexes" (stronger defenses).

Along the same line, Jung's Self has been described as bestowing unconditional love, wisdom, and healing power, attributes of the heart. And, in the process of individuation, the healthy ego (that utilizes the pre-frontals) begins to communicate and align with the Self/heart. Then, the attributes of the Self can inform and shine through all of the ego's choices and actions. Is that not reflective of the heart-pre-frontal connection that allows the new brain to overrule the instinctual drives of the old brains? Pearce goes on to say, "At every conception or stage nature asks: Will we be able to move into the higher realms of intelligence this time, or must we defend ourselves again?" Or, will we choose to see through the perceptual lens of love, or will we remain in the perceptual lens of fear?

The yogis also talked about the pull of opposing forces. In the preface to *The Bhagavad Gita,* translated by Eknath Easwaran, Easwaran states, "Two forces pervade human life, the Gita says: the upward thrust of evolution and the downward pull of our evolutionary past… The struggle is between two halves of human nature, and choices are posed every moment." This corresponds with the heart-prefrontal neural circuitry (evolving/choice) versus the amygdala-reptilian neural circuitry (regressive/reactive). The heart is given a special place in the yogic tradition. The yogis and mystics have always acknowledged the heart as the seat of the Self.

In the chakra system, the Heart chakra is the transitional chakra between the ego-oriented, lower chakras, and the Self-oriented, higher chakras, and is considered the doorway to higher consciousness. In fact, in yogic meditation, we are often instructed to focus on the heart or the third eye as we repeat our mantra. That sounds a lot like activating the heart and the prefrontal lobes to me! Yoga not only encourages focusing on the heart, there are a multitude of breathing, asana, and meditation practices geared to the heart chakra and designed to open the chest and activate the heart. Andrew Harvey and Karuna Erickson have a book entitled, *Heart Yoga*, the Sacred Marriage of Yoga and Mysticism.

Knowing all of this, how do we access and strengthen the heart-prefrontal connection? The key lies in learning ways to activate and energize the heart, and build new neural circuitry patterns. Before moving into the practices and techniques that address the heart, let's consider the HeartMath research on positive emotional states. As stated, their research showed that positive emotional states (love, care, appreciation, awe, reverence, gratitude), have the ability to regulate heart rhythm patterns and bring them into a coherent state. This synchronizes the heart, brain, and nervous system, and creates a balanced psychophysiological (mind/emotion/body) state. This coherent state has far reaching effects. In addition to turning on our cell's self-healing capacities, it balances the autonomic nervous system; accesses our intuitive, heart intelligence; and builds new neural circuitry from the heart to the prefrontal cortex, and in the area of the prefrontal cortex that registers positive emotions. We create this coherent state by *activating* the heart and *experiencing* positive emotional states. HeartMath researchers developed this technique.

EXERCISE

> Step1. **Heart Focus**. Focus your attention in the area of your heart or the center of your chest. You may want to put your hand on the center of your chest to help you keep your focus there. If your mind wanders, just keep shifting your attention back to your heart.
>
> Step 2. **Heart Breathing**. As you focus on the area of your heart, feel your breath flowing in and out through that area. Breathe slowly and gently in and out through your heart and do this until your breathing feels smooth and balanced. Find a natural inner rhythm that feels good to you.
>
> Step 3. **Heart Feeling**. Continue to breathe through your heart. As you do so, elicit an image or a memory that evokes a positive feeling, such as a time when you felt an inner sense of well-being or something warmed your heart. Use your senses fully to evoke and experience the positive feeling. This could be appreciation or love toward a special person or pet, a place in nature that inspires awe, or doing something that you thoroughly enjoy. Take the time to really *feel* appreciation, care, well-being, awe, enjoyment.

The Quick Coherence technique takes only moments to do, and therefore, can be fit into even the busiest of days. It can be done often. It is especially effective just before falling asleep at night, and as you awake in the morning. In the Heart Feeling step, it is important that you evoke the feelings and feel them; don't just think about them. When stressed, if you do the Quick Coherence technique and change your heart rhythm to a more coherent pattern, your feelings and perceptions will change.

There are other practices that connect us to our hearts and engender positive emotional states. One practice that evokes a positive emotional state and then sustains it, has been around since the *Yoga Sutras.* This is the practice of maitri, most often translated as "loving-kindness". The Buddhist equivalent is metta, which has also been translated as "unconditional friendliness".

EXERCISE

> In this practice begin by setting the intention in your mind for your own happiness and for the happiness of all others. As Sharon Salzberg, author of the book, *Lovingkindness*, states, "The intention is enough. We form the intention in our mind for our happiness and the happiness of all. This is different from struggling to fabricate a certain feeling, to create it out of our will."
>
> After setting the intention, quiet your mind... deepen your breath... relax your body... and then start repeating a series of phrases. Here is one example:
>
> May I be free from danger.
> May I be mentally happy.
> May I be physically happy.
> May I live in peace and have ease of well-being.
>
> Repeat the metta phrases, offering a kind and gentle friendship to yourself. Then direct the phrases and wishes to others, as in, "Just as I want to be happy, so do you want to be happy. May you be free from danger..." In the "you" category, start with benefactors, loved ones and dear friends, repeating the phrases for each person inserting their names. Next, move to neutral people in your life, repeating the phrases for them. Finally, the most difficult people in your life, even those you might consider the "enemy".
>
> After the "you" wishes, repeat the phrases for "we". "May we be free from danger... " The final category is the wishes and offers of friendship to "all beings". "May all beings be free from danger... "

As a meditation practice this can be done for 20 to 30 minutes or longer. Through this practice we grow to feel and sustain these positive emotions, soften and open our hearts, and send good wishes out into our environment and to the collective consciousness. This is powerful because energy follows intention.

Perhaps the most challenging aspect of the metta practice is sending loving-kindness to the difficult people in our lives, especially those who we feel have harmed us. For this, use the forgiveness meditation. Salzberg describes it as follows in her book, *Lovingkindness*:

EXERCISE

> If I have hurt or harmed anyone, knowingly or unknowingly, I ask their forgiveness. I ask your (a name can be inserted) forgiveness.
>
> If anyone has hurt or harmed me, knowingly or unknowingly, I forgive them. _____, I forgive you.
>
> For all the ways I have hurt or harmed myself, knowingly or unknowingly, I offer forgiveness to myself. May I be filled with loving-kindness toward myself and others.
>
> Here again, the intention is enough, especially at the beginning. Forgiveness is an essential feature of healing our hearts, our bodies, and our lives, and we must forgive both ourselves and others.

EXERCISE

> Another practice that relates to a core heart feeling is the practice of gratitude.
>
> Begin a daily gratitude journal. Each morning write in the journal three things you are grateful for and will practice gratitude for that day. At the end of your entry you can say to yourself, "What a blessing it is to be alive today."
>
> It may seem simple, but it is extremely powerful, as it establishes an "attitude of gratitude" that begins to pervade your entire life, even during times when your life is challenging.

It's been said that the degree of our happiness reflects the size of the gap between what our heart knows and what we actually do. It is essential that we move from the head to the heart; from "you have to be reasonable" to "follow your heart". We know how to develop and attune to our minds. Now we must also develop and attune to our hearts. The fourth practice involves listening to your heart.

EXERCISE

> Your yearnings, your longings, your dreams, and your passions are the ways that your heart speaks to you. The heart is the source of your guiding wisdom and intuitive intelligence, as well as, their voice. Develop the habit of asking your heart for intuitive guidance.
>
> This involves a movement from the head to the heart as you increasingly identify with and are guided by your heart, not just your analytical mind.
>
> When you have a question or a dilemma, close your eyes, quiet your mind, drop into your heart and ask your heart for the right response or action. Then stay still and wait…an answer will come. Learning to trust your heart-felt senses will enable you to become more resourceful.

The final practice has to do with taking yourself into your own heart with compassion and acceptance; an extension of the loving-kindness practice. One method of this practice is what Richard Moss calls "sacred attention," introduced in Chapter One. It refers to the quality of attention we offer ourselves. We view ourselves, and our experiences through the eyes of the heart and the lens of unconditional love. Brugh Joy taught that there is no judgment in the Heart Center. The heart appreciates and reveres whatever is in front of it because it understands its connection to the whole. It holds all those pairs of opposites that we discussed earlier, and truly loves unconditionally.

Interestingly, Pearce speaks in his book about the heart-brain connection, and the fact that the heart is neurally connected with every facet of the body and brain but has no neural complex for making judgments. Judging is assigned to the heart's "servant," the brain. Sacred attention allows us to be with all parts of ourselves, the good, the bad, and the ugly, with tender, loving acceptance. This leads to the experience of divine love, channeled through the Self to the self, which is unconditional and unbounded. As Andrew Harvey says, "What all of us could live if we allowed the overwhelming love of God to come to us." This may be the most transformational practice of all.

As we open our hearts and remove the obstacles to our true nature, we become more loving and compassionate human beings. We begin to intuitively know what really matters, and that is love. We increasingly know that love must begin with love and acceptance of ourselves, with lovingly taking ourselves into our own hearts. Then, we can truly offer love, compassion, and acceptance to others. This awareness begins to inform all of our choices and actions. We instinctively know that we are one with all that is, and we want to increasingly give, love, and serve all beings and life itself.

This, for me, is what the global shift in consciousness is all about. It is, in part, about our awakening to our true selves, our Essence, which is pure consciousness. It is an evolutionary process of consciousness becoming aware of its self, and continuing to evolve and be embodied. And, it is about the movement from the head to the heart, from the love of power to the power of love, from the fear-based, survival instincts of the reptilian/limbic brain to the love-based choices of the heart/prefrontal cortex.

At this point in our history, with our world facing so many potential threats to life as we know it, can we birth a transformation of consciousness? We are again, as a species, being asked if we will be able to move into the higher realms of intelligence this time, or must we defend ourselves again? It is up to us to do our part to make the shift into the heart, and to live our lives accordingly. This requires that we do the work of addressing emotional wounds and negative or limiting beliefs, so we can break down the defenses that have hardened our hearts. These walls around our hearts kept us safe, we thought, but often at the price of being disconnected from ourselves and others. We must do the heart practices so we can open our hearts to ourselves and others, transforming ourselves and our world in the process.

Chapter Seven: The Transformed Life
Embodying and Living It

In the last chapter we addressed the heart as a key to transformation. We explored the practices that enable us to access and open our hearts so we can be informed and guided by the heart's intuitive wisdom. Heart work always comes down to unconditional love and compassion. This process starts with love and compassion for ourselves, and expands to love of others, and all of life. Ultimately, we open ourselves and surrender to the overwhelming love of the divine. We **experience** feeling loved and supported, guided and protected by a loving, creative intelligence that is summoning us forward on our evolutionary journey. We come to embrace "the magnificence and the mystery", and fall in love with Life – "the full catastrophe".

That **experience** is what is transformational. We prepare for and invite that experience of divine love through our psychospiritual practices and healing work. I have presented numerous practices and techniques in this book. The critical part is finding the ones that work for you, and then, practicing them consistently. We must do as the masters have said: "practice, practice, practice". The importance of this cannot be stressed enough. It is not what we know, but what we do. It is consistent effort that leads to the grace of transformation.

In Chapter One I presented the eight limbs of Raja Yoga, the "royal road" to Self-realization. Limb one is the yamas, or the restraints. As taught by Swami Rami, they help us "regain balance in our lives and support us in having healthy relationships with our self, others, and all of life." The yamas are ahimsa (non-harming), satya (truthfulness), asteya (non-stealing), brahmacharya (moderation of the senses), and aparigraha (non-possessiveness). We intentionally seek to practice these restraints as they remove obstacles to our healing and growth. At the same time, as we do the work to shift our consciousness, the restraints naturally become part of who we are. Limb two is the niyamas, or observances. The first two are saucha (purity) and santosha (contentment). They remind us "of the value of cleansing and properly nourishing the body and mind, and of the benefit of accepting what comes into our lives, and releasing what leaves our lives, so that we can be content."

The last three of the five niyamas are tapas, svadhyaya, and ishvara pranidhana, and are essential pieces of the puzzle. As I learned them through the Himalayan Tradition, as taught by Swami Rama, they are observances that are essential to this process. Tapas means "heat" and it implies effort. When we make a disciplined effort, we build energy and enthusiasm for our task. Tapas is the self-discipline that leads to self-mastery. Svadhyaya is Self-study, which is the study of the Self, the Infinite dwelling in the finite. Through mantra repetition, a teacher's words, and reading, Self-study inspires us to the Self. Finally, ishvara pranidhana is self-surrender. By learning to trust in the guidance and grace of the Infinite, we allow the diminishment of the ego, and the tensions and burdens of ego are washed off. **After our own full effort, grace enters."**

Having stressed the relationship between effort and grace, I want to share one more of Joan Borysenko's stories. Her wit and wisdom have always captivated me. She told of having dinner with a friend and their discussion about how difficult it was to change a long standing pattern in one's life. Her friend reached for the bread knife and laid it on top of an outstretched finger, making a symbolic see-saw. The friend then said, "We work and work to shift a pattern and nothing much seems to change". She had begun slowly moving the bread knife over her finger as a see-saw would move. She continued, "Then, all of a sudden everything shifts," as the knife comes down to the table on the other side of her finger. "The first 51 % is our effort; the other 49% is God's matching grant of grace."

Even as we heal, enlarge our personality, and align more and more with the Self, as long as we are in a body, here on this plain, we are still human and subject to our human frailties. I love the master's definition of the "perfect disciple" that Deepak Chopra quoted in *How to Know God*. It was, "The one who is stumbling always, but never falls." It is important in this process to never loose touch with "the embarrassment of being human". Healing and transformation are not about goodness or perfection, but rather **wholeness**.

Jung's process of individuation is about becoming whole, and also involves effort, courage, and steadfastness, especially as it relates to addressing our shadow selves and their unhealed emotions. Sue Monk Kidd, in *When the Heart Waits*, speaks of this process relating some memorable lines from Arthur Miller's *After the Fall* that speaks to the dilemma of those banished parts of us. Miller writes, "I had the same dream each night – that I had a child, and even in the dream I saw that the child was my life; and it was an idiot, and I ran away. Until I thought, if I could kiss it…perhaps I could rest. And, I bent to its broken face, and it was horrible… but I kissed it. I think one must finally take one's life in one's arms".

Kidd goes on to say, "In facing the many banished parts of ourselves, that's exactly what we need to do; bend down to the broken, horrible faces in ourselves and kiss each one". We find that as we own and integrate the split-off and fragmented parts of ourselves we become more whole and authentic. And, as we pull back our projections from others, we not only heal ourselves, we heal our relationships. Shadow work is one of the most important practices we can do today, both for ourselves, our relationships, and the collective.

Another challenging part of this process of individuation is opening to and engaging with life – all of it, the light and the dark, the pleasure and the pain. I think that John A. Sanford, an Episcopalian priest and Jungian analyst, describes it so well in his book *Healing and Wholeness*. He states, "Good and evil will be curiously intermingled in any meaningful life process. If we are to become whole, life will send us, not what we want, but what we need in order to grow. The forces of evil will have to touch our lives for without the dark Luciferian power, consciousness does not emerge… Individuation is a work, a life opus, a task that calls upon us not to avoid life's difficulties and dangers, but to perceive the meaning in the pattern of events that form our lives".

This is deep work, but it *is* the adventure of a lifetime. I am reminded of May Sarton's poem, *The Invocation to Kali* in which she writes, "Help us to be the always hopeful gardeners of the spirit who know that without darkness nothing comes to birth as without light nothing flowers". The journey to wholeness requires self-discipline, Self-study, and self-surrender. It asks us to embrace the uncertain and the unknown, and to hang out in that territory for indefinite periods of time. It confronts us with our humanness, the light and the dark, and it delights us with our divinity.

During the dark times we are gifted with what I have called "compensatory grace". After our effort, the grace of transformation comes. In my personal journey I have found that during those dark and challenging times when I have felt alone and bereft, in hindsight, I saw that the universe was doing for me what I could not do for myself. As Sanford knew, life was giving me what I needed to get to the next stage in my transformative process. We are truly supported in this journey whether we know it or not.

Apollo astronaut Edgar Mitchell had a numinous experience when he saw the earth floating in space as the spacecraft he was in was returning from the moon. Upon his return he decided to leave NASA, and he founded the Institute for the Noetic Sciences (IONS). IONS' mission is to advance the science of consciousness and human experience to serve individual and collective transformation. They have been a leader in promoting and doing cutting edge research in the areas of emerging paradigms, human capacities, and integral health and healing.

Through this research, they developed a model of consciousness transformation. Their findings were published in the book, *Living Deeply: The Art and Science of Transformation in Everyday Life*. They found that an integral part of the transformational process was discovering and doing a set of practices. In an article on the book by Cassandra Vieten, Ph. D., Director of Research at IONS, she states, "These practices can take many forms but include four essential elements: *attention* toward greater self-awareness; *intention* toward healing outcomes; *repetition* of new behaviors; and *guidance* from trusted people who are experienced in the practice".

It was also reported in *Living Deeply* that the result of committed practice over time is the transformation of consciousness. Part of this, is the tendency to develop a belief system and lifestyle that manifests the transformed life in the following three ways: The first, is that our life, itself, becomes our spiritual practice. This is most evident in our choosing to live our lives consciously and mindfully; seeking to align all our choices and actions with our intentions, and with what we say we value and believe. This applies not just to the big decisions, but to the multitude of choices we make each and every day. Jung believed we each have the choice to live our lives consciously or unconsciously. By consciously, he meant, listening to our inner guiding wisdom, and learning to live authentically, with heart. This would inevitably lead us to our destiny, where we feel centered and connected to our Essence. For Jung, fate is a life lived unconsciously, our choices made as if we have no choice, or for reasons that exclude what our heart wants us to consider. A transformed life leads us to our destiny, and enables us to fulfill our unique purpose and potential.

Gary Zukav reminds us in *The Seat of the Soul*, "At each moment you choose the intentions that will shape your experiences, and those things upon which you will focus your attention. If you choose unconsciously, you evolve unconsciously. If you choose consciously, you evolve consciously." One final quote that speaks to what is involved in living consciously is by Richard Moss. He states, "Consciousness is a great privilege. But consciousness is also an obligation, the obligation to live in ever deepening relationship. The on-going invitation of life is to go beyond the threshold of our fears, beyond the boundaries of who or what we think we are. Instead of living from our smaller, contracted self which in seeking for security chooses to remain separate, we are forever invited into our larger self which is already in profound relationship with all that is". That is a transformed life.

Living Deeply's second way we manifest the shift in consciousness is that we move from a "me" to a "we" mentality; we increasingly release self-interest and self-aggrandizement, and focus instead on the welfare of all. We become a "citizen of the universe", and respect the entire web of life, knowing we live in an interdependent universe. Two traditional schools of yoga are Hinayana yoga and Mahayana yoga. The goal of Hinayana is Self-realization which I have focused on. What complements and grows out of Self-realization is the path of Mahayana, the goal of which is the release from suffering of all sentient beings. When we achieve the experience of Self, in that experience, we know we are all Self, so what we want for ourselves we want for all.

As Einstein said, "The idea of separateness is an optical delusion of consciousness." In reality, there *is* only one of us here. Knowing this, not just in our head, but in our gut, changes everything. We shift from self-interest and "what's in it for me?" to a desire to promote the greater good and "how can I serve?" Our practice may shift to the metta or loving-kindness meditation that I discussed in the last chapter. In this practice, our desire is for the liberation of all beings. "May all beings be safe, happy, and free" This desire begins to inform all of our choices, all of our actions, and all of our relationships. Lynne Twist's book, *The Soul of Money*, is an excellent exploration of our relationship with money. I once was struck by a bumper sticker that said, "Live simply so others can simply live." We increasingly seek to bring all aspects of our lives into, what is referred to as, "right relationship."

Pandit Rajmani Tigunait, the Spiritual Head of the Himalayan Institute that was founded by Swami Rama, and a student of Swami Rama's, told this story in an Institute publication. He shared that having practiced diligently and consistently for many, many years, he was disturbed by his failure to understand the source of his periodic anger and sadness so he put his concern before Swami Rama. Swami Rama replied, "The source of your problem lies in the vast field of the collective consciousness. Millions of people pass the night with hunger. Billions struggle day and night just to barely remain alive. The anger and grief oozing from their pores has seeped into the entire web of life. Their sorrow has penetrated the building blocks of our life – food, water and air... More than 5 million children every year die of malnutrition. Forty million HIV/AIDS patients are simply left at the mercy of a slow death. Like mini-factories, these billions of hearts are pouring clouds of pain and agony, fear and insecurity, and anger and violence into the planet's atmosphere. These clouds travel all around the globe influencing the hearts and minds of everyone, including those who appear to be far removed from the destitute.

Like it or not, you cannot find and secure your personal happiness in isolation from the happiness of others. Today's spirituality demands that we find ways to make the external world conducive to our inner journey, and the social atmosphere conducive to our personal transformation... Travel deep into the core of your being. There you will hear that today spirituality demands that we make a commitment to share, serve and make a difference. That is the only way."

Here again the new science is confirming and validating what the yogis have taught for years and years. The Global Coherence Initiative (GCI), founded in the summer of 2008 by the Institute of HeartMath, has brought together noted scientists, researchers, and leaders in many fields to facilitate a global shift in consciousness. GCI is a science-based initiative to unite millions of people in heart-focused care and intention to shift global consciousness from instability, stress, and discord, to balance, cooperation, and enduring peace. In an article on the GCI Website, written by Annette Deyhle, Ph.D. and Rollin McCraty, Ph.D. of GCI, they talk about GCI's three major hypotheses.

They state, "Hypothesis No. 1: All living things are interconnected, and we communicate with each other via biological and electromagnetic fields. Hypothesis No. 2: Not only are humans affected by planetary energetic fields, but conversely the earth's energetic systems are also influenced by collective human emotions and consciousness. Much of the planetary field environment is made up of the collective consciousness of the inhabitants." Sounds a lot like what Swami Rama was talking about.

Research done at Princeton University for the Global Consciousness Project revealed that data collected by magnetometers on two National Oceanic and Atmospheric Administration (NOAA) space weather satellites supported the hypothesis that collective human emotion interacts with and modulates the earth's magnetic field.

This leads to their third hypothesis which I quote as follows: "Hypothesis No. 3: Large numbers of people intentionally creating heart-coherent states of care, love, compassion, and appreciation can generate a coherent standing wave that will help offset the current planetary wave of stress, discord, and incoherence." The GCI Project, which is worldwide, is currently orchestrating that very thing. You can learn about GCI by going to their website which is listed in the Resource Section. These are examples that show the significance and potential impact of shifting from a "me" to a "we" mentality. A transformed life can create a transformed world.

Finally, the third manifestation of the shift in consciousness described in *Living Deeply* is that we see the divinity in everyone and every thing. We see the sacred in all of creation. Again, if the Self we experience in Self-realization is divine, and we are all Selves, then we are all divine. This is referred to as the Divine Immanent, or the divine indwelling the finite. If we really believed and lived this, how would our relationship with our self be different…with others, especially those we judge…with nature and all of creation? Could we continue to make war or destroy other species and the environment? This is a shift that, like the others, entails a movement into the heart, and a willingness to see through the eyes of the Self, which is through the eyes of love.

IONS produced a CD that was a recording of an interview they did with Andrew Harvey. In the interview Harvey talked about sacred activism, which I will address in the Epilogue, and about some of the changes that need to occur at this time. He spoke of the need to ask for the eyes to see and the heart to feel the sacredness of reality. If, however, we do wake up to this, we then also wake up to the heartbreak of reality, which is the response to what we are doing to all of this sacredness. He calls this "an initiation into radical heartbreak," and believes this is what is needed if we are to transform ourselves and our world.

This willingness to experience "an initiation into radical heartbreak", to have our hearts broken open, is also a manifestation of the shift from fragmented to whole. We become open to *being with* all of life, including the dark and uncomfortable parts. This could also be called a shift from an "either/or" to a "both/and" mentality. We embrace the polarities that are inherent in life, and hold the tension of the opposites, rather than choose one side and banish and project the other. We open to experiencing life, and in so doing, sanctify it.

Oriah Mountain Dreamer talks about this beautifully in the Introduction to her book, *The Invitation*. She states, "I find little comfort or guidance in traditional dogma or unqualified New Age optimism. Because beneath the small daily trials are harder paradoxes, things the mind cannot reconcile but the heart must hold if we are to live fully: profound tiredness and radical hope; shattered beliefs and relentless faith; the seemingly contradictory longings for personal freedom and a deep commitment to others, for solitude and intimacy... Life lived intimately may not be easier. But it is fuller, richer, and more open to everything: the confusion and the insight, the excitement and the boredom, the shadow and the light." To open our hearts to the "suchness" of life, and declare an unconditional "yes" to it all, may be one of the most challenging parts of the shift to wholeness, but it rewards us with a life fully and richly lived.

I cannot end the discussion on wholeness without coming full circle to where we began. In the Introduction to the book, I stated that all three perspectives, the ancient wisdom of yoga, transpersonal psychology, and the new science, offer a holistic approach to healing and transformation. I proposed that we needed to address the whole person or we risk missing an essential piece of the puzzle. And, since we are multi-dimensional beings, we need practices and tools that address the mind, emotion, body, and spirit. My hope is that I have offered that to you. Certain types of practices will appeal more to you, and you will be willing to practice them more consistently. Most of the practices that I have presented address multiple dimensions simultaneously. Just remember not to ignore any area: mind, emotion, body or spirit for they are interrelated, and all affect each other.

A very powerful part of my personal journey has been doing holotropic and integrative breathwork. Part of what makes it so powerful is that it is an experience that incorporates and heals the mind, emotion, body and spirit. It *is* important that the work be done with a reputable and trained facilitator. Both holotropic breathwork, developed by Stan Grof, M.D. and integrative breathwork, developed by Jacquelyn Small, offer training and certification programs. There is information on this in the Resource section. Accessing non-ordinary states of consciousness, which can be done through many of the practices in this book, is an essential part of healing and transformation. As Einstein suggested, we can't solve a problem at the same level of consciousness that created it.

We *can* heal and transform ourselves and our lives. Then, by embodying and living the transformed life, we become agents of change in our world. We become part of the critical mass that can shift the collective consciousness and transform our world. Let us now look at what this global shift in consciousness entails.

Epilogue: The Love of Power to the Power of Love
The Global Shift and the Call to Sacred Activism

As I've been saying throughout the book, this shift in consciousness that we have been exploring is not just a personal one, but a global one, as well. We are in the midst of a paradigm shift that is about a transformation in consciousness, and an evolutionary movement to a higher level of consciousness for the species. It has been referred to as a paradigm shift of the magnitude of the one that took us from the Dark Ages to the Middle Ages. I would like to briefly address some of what is being said about this paradigm shift.

Through our evolutionary process we have moved into what is being called the age of consciousness, and its world view is slowly replacing the old scientific-materialistic world view which has been dominant for the past 400 years. Some say we are moving from our adolescence as a species into our adulthood. Anodea Judith, Ph.D., in her book, *Waking the Global Heart*, refers to the shift as a movement from the power paradigm, representing the love of power and the third chakra energies, to the heart paradigm representing the power of love and the fourth or heart chakra energies. Edmund Bourne, Ph.D.'s book, *Global Shift*, is another great resource on this topic. In his book he talks about the differences in these paradigms. Some of the differences in what these world views value and espouse are as follows:

Power Paradigm	**Heart Paradigm**
Militarism	Peace and social justice
Competition	Co-creation and collaboration
Growth and expansion	Sustainability
Either/or (duality/separation)	Both/and (unity/whole)
Mind over body (head)	Mind-body-spirit integration (heart)
Exploitation of nature	Deep ecology
I-it (object)	I-Thou-We (all subjects)
Ego-driven/individually focused	Relationship-driven/collectively focused |//
I will add:	
Masculine dominated	Partnership (masculine and feminine)
Ego driven	Ego aligned with Self
Amygdala/reptilian	Heart/pre-frontal
Fear based	Love based

There are many signs that this shift is already occurring. One example is the Global Coherence Initiative that I discussed in the last chapter. They are just one of a number of different groups facilitating global intention projects. Another example is the Peace Alliance. The Peace Alliance is a grassroots movement in this country to support the passage of Congressman Dennis Kucinich's house bill (H.R. 808) that would create a cabinet level Department of Peace in our government.

The emerging shift in world view is accompanied by a corresponding shift in personal values, in what we deem to be important. These new values share a common feature: a movement away from a materialistic to a humanitarian-spiritual orientation toward life. Some of the new values are as follows:

Reverence for nature and the earth
A sense of inclusiveness for all humanity
Compassion
Integration of the Feminine
Valuing intuition
Voluntary simplicity
Respect for being present (conscious, mindful)
The primacy of unconditional love

A growing momentum of people and institutions are embracing this new path, and they are now connecting, to ultimately form a worldwide web. What we believe and do matters. We can be part of that critical mass needed to shift the collective consciousness. As Jimi Hendrix said, "When the power of love overcomes the love of power, the world will know peace." We must ask ourselves, "Where am I in terms of my world view and my values? Are my intentions and actions aligned with the Heart Paradigm and its values?

Some propose that our survival as a species depends on whether or not the collective makes this paradigm shift. There are scientists that are saying the planet is deep into its sixth mass destruction – this time, the direct result of human behavior. We are facing great peril. To hide our heads in the sand is dangerous, so is a blind optimism or refusal to acknowledge the collective shadow and the dark, Luciferian forces at work. The collapse of the world's financial markets, the potential outcomes of our refusal to address our destruction of the environment, and the very real threat of a nuclear war are sobering to say the least. We simply cannot afford "business as usual". Some say that if we do not change, we will not make it another 50 years.

Time is of the essence and "affairs are now soul-sized". We would do well to heed the words of Christopher Fry, which I first read in the Introduction of Jacquelyn Small's book, *Awakening in Time.* Fry writes:

Thank God our time is now when wrong
Comes up to meet us everywhere,
Never to leave us till we take
The longest stride of soul men ever took.
Affairs are now soul-sized.
The enterprise is exploration into God.
Where are you making for?
It takes so many thousand years to wake.
But will you wake for pity's sake?

These very threats, when faced, can provide the impetus for transformation. It starts with the personal and evolves into the collective. We must do both. Our spiritual evolution requires it. In their book on Heart Rhythm Meditation called *Living from the Heart*, Puran and Susanna Bair discuss the difference between upward and downward meditation. They state, "Upward meditation corresponds to the transcendent view that the physical world is an illusion that, in myriad forms, covers an underlying unity. When, through meditation, you escape the artificial boundaries imposed by individual identity, you discover your connection to a greater dimension of yourself (Samadhi)…

The development of downward meditation required a breakthrough that occurred later… Instead of seeing the physical world as an illusion that masks the true reality, we now understand the physical world to be the point of it all, the ultimate objective of all reality, the culmination of divine intention". This leads us to what Andrew Harvey and others are calling sacred activism. Harvey refers to it as "when the joy of compassionate service is married to a practical and pragmatic drive to transform all existing economic, social, and political institutions, a radical and potentially all-transforming holy force is born. This radical holy force is sacred activism".

Harvey goes on to say in his book, *The Hope*, "What I pray that the vision of Sacred Activism will give you, is the vision and the hope that will enable you to go through danger and difficulty with a tender heart, a peaceful mind, an increasingly supple and loving body, and a passionate, restless hunger to do all you can to preserve human and animal life on earth. I hope it will inspire you to help bring forth a new humanity and new world". He believes we can only do this by radically transforming ourselves. Interestingly, the transformation he refers to involves the heart, mind, body, and spirit, and reminds us of the work to be done in each of those areas. We transform ourselves so that we can become vessels through which the loving, creative intelligence of the universe can flow, and become transmitters of unconditional love in this world. One way that this love is manifested is through service. In the yogic tradition it is called "seva", which is selfless service.

Finally, Harvey shows us wherein the hope is found. He states, "You come to the end of your fantasy that the Divine is there to give *you* what *you* want. Slowly, painfully, but with more and more authentic hope and authentic joy, you start to suspect that we are here, not to bask in God's love, but willingly, freely and with answering love – to give all we have to Love's work of transformation so Love can transform all we have, all we are, to gold… It is in surrendering to this greatest of all laws of alchemy that we discover and *become* the real gold, the real power, the real hope".

I came across this statement: "Imagine a world where leaders' decisions are heart-felt and guided by conscious thoughtfulness; a world where societies benefit from intuitive, collective wisdom, and where scientific discovery and technological innovation is derived from heart-centered minds". **The task before us is to hold the vision of a new earth and an enlightened world, and to be change agents and midwives of the birthing of a new paradigm. We only have to do our part, but our part is so very critical.** As Ghandi said, "be the change you wish to see happen." As each of us transforms ourselves and does our part, we become part of the solution, rather than part of the problem. "If not now, when? If not you, who?" Harvey suggests that we ask ourselves daily, "How did I help today to mid-wife this new humanity?"

I recently heard Jean Houston say, in regards to the environmental crises in the Gulf of Mexico, "Crises are a masterpiece of possibilities." We must die to the old in order to birth the new, and a birthing process is never without pain and danger. Like the Chinese pictograph symbols for the word "crisis" (danger and opportunity), all crises inherently contain both danger and opportunity. Our current global crises are offering us the opportunity to create a new humanity and a just, peaceful and sustainable earth.

Houston expressed feeling very hopeful, and that she believes that the grass roots can do it. Hopefully, this book has provided some support in moving you forward in your journey of healing and transformation, and may the merits of all our effort be of benefit to all beings. I want to thank Joan Borysenko and the Yoga Warehouse in Fort Lauderdale for two of my favorite metta phrases. May we all hold these loving-kindness intentions in our hearts:

May we be at peace.
May our hearts remain open.
May we know the beauty of our own true selves.
May we be whole and a source of wholeness in this world.

And may this be so for all beings.

May the whole world attain peace and harmony.
May the whole world attain peace and happiness.
And, may that peace begin within each of our hearts.

Namaste.

Recommended Reading and Resources

Introduction

David Richo, *The Power of Coincidence* (Boston: Shambhala, 2007)
Norman Cousins, *Anatomy of an Illness* (New York: WW Norton, 1979)
    Head First: the Biology of Hope (New York: Penguin, 1989)
Joseph Campbell, *The Hero with a Thousand Faces* (Novato: New World Library, 2008)

Chapter One

Peter Russell, *The Global Brain* (New York: J.P. Tarcher, 1983)
S. Anderson and R. Sovic, *Yoga, Mastering the Basics* (Himalayan Institute, 2000)
www.himalayaninstitute.org
Swami Rama, *The Royal Path* (Himalayan Institute Press, 1998)
Kathleen Brehony, *Awakening At Midlife* (New York: Riverhead Books, 1996)
Erik Erickson, *Childhood and Society* (New York: WW Norton, 1963)
Lynne McTaggart, *The Field* (New York: Harper Collins, 2002)
Richard Moss, *The Mandala of Being* (Novato: New World Library, 2007)
S. Salzberg and J. Goldstein, *Insight Meditation* (workbook), (Sounds True, 2001)
Roberto Assagioli, *Psychosynthesis* (New York: Viking Press, 1965)
Dan Siegel, *The Mindful Brain* (New York: Norton and Co., 2007)

Chapter Two

Timothy McCall, *Yoga as Medicine* (New York: Bantam Dell, 2007)
Rudolph Ballentine, *Radical Healing* (New York: Harmony Books, 1999)
    Diet and Nutrition (Himalayan Institute Press, 1978)
Yoga International Reprint Series, *Simply Breathing* and *Breathing Lessons*
S. Rama, R. Ballentine, A. Hymes, *Science of Breath* (Himalayan Institute, 1979)
Jack Lee Rosenberg, *Body, Self and Soul* (Atlanta: Humanics Limited, 1985)
J. Conger, *Jung and Reich: The Body as Shadow* (Berkeley: N. Atlantic, 2005)
Eugene Gendlin, *Focusing* (New York: Everest House, 1978)
    Focusing Oriented Psychotherapy (New York: Guilford, 1996)
Candice Pert, *The Molecules of Emotion* (New York: Touchstone, 1997)
Christiane Northrup, *Women's Bodies, Women's Wisdom* (New York: Bantam, 1994)

Chapter Three

Anodea Judith, *Wheels of Life* (St. Paul: Llewellyn Publications, 1995)
    Eastern Body Western Mind (Berkeley: Celestial Arts, 1996)
Caroline Myss, *Anatomy of the Spirit* (New York: Three Rivers Press, 1996)

Ambika Wauters, *Chakras and Their Archetypes* (Freedom: Crossing Press, 1999)
John Ruskan, *Emotional Clearing* (New York: R. Wyler & Co., 1993)
Richard Gerber, *Vibrational Medicine* (Santa Fe: Bear & Co., 1988)
Stan Grof, *The Adventure of Self Discovery* (Albany: SUNY Press, 1988)
Erik Erikson, *Childhood and Society* (New York: WW Norton, 1963)
W. Brugh Joy, *Joy's Way* (New York: Putnam Book, 1979)
Dawson Church, *The Genie in Your Genes* (Santa Rosa: Elite Books, 2007)
Julia Cameron, *The Artist's Way* (New York: Putnam's Sons, 1992)
Robert A. Johnson, *Inner Work* (San Francisco: HarperCollins, 1986)
Jeremy Taylor, *Dream Work* (New York: Paulist Press, 1983)
Eugene Gendlin, *Let Your Body Interpret Your Dreams*, (Wilmette: Chiron, 1986)
Dawson Church, *The Genie in Your Genes* (Santa Rosa: Elite Books, 2007)
John Sarno, *The Mindbody Perscription* (New York: Warner Books, 1998)
Stephen Cope, *Yoga and the Quest for the True Self* (New York: Bantam, 1999)

Chapter Four

Gary Kraftsow, *Yoga for Wellness* (New York: Penguin Group, 1999)
D. Childre and D. Rozman, *Transforming Depression* (Oakland: New Harbinger, 2007)
www.heartmath.com
www.heartmath.org
Deepak Chopra, *The Book of Secrets* (New York: Harmony Books, 2004)
Herbert Benson, *The Relaxation Response* (New York: HarperCollins, 1975)
Gregg Braden, *The Spontaneous Healing of Belief* (New York: Hay House, 2008)
R. Callahan and J. Callahan, *Thought Field Therapy and Trauma*
www.emofree.com
Tapas Fleming, *You Can Heal Now: The Tapas Acupressure Technique*
Fred Gallo, *Energy Psychology* (Boca Raton: CRC Press, 1999)
www.energypsych.org

Chapter Five

Bruce Lipton, *The Biology of Belief* (Santa Rosa: Elite Books, 2005)
Dawson Church, *The Genie in Your Genes* (Santa Rosa: Elite Books, 2007)
A. Ellis, R. Harper, *A Guide to Rational Living* (Englewood Cliffs: Wilshire Book, 1975)
David Burns, *Feeling Good Handbook* (New York: Penguin Books, 1989)
J.S. Beck, *Cognitive Therapy: Basics and Beyond* (New York: Guilford Press)
S Hayes, K. Strosahl, K. Wilson, *Acceptance and Commitment Therapy* (New York: Guilford Press, 1999)
M. Linehan, *Cognitive-behavioral Therapy for Borderline Personality Disorder* (1993)
Prabhavananda, C. Isherwood (Sutras), *How to Know God* (Hollywood: Vedanta, 1981)

Nischala Joy Devi, (Sutras), *The Secret Power of Yoga* (New York: Three Rivers, 2007)
S. Anderson and R. Sovic, *Yoga, Mastering the Basics* (Himalayan Institute, 2000)
Lawrence LeShan, *How to Meditate* (New York: Bantam Books, 1974)
Jon Kabat-Zinn, *Wherever You Go, There You Are* (New York: Hyperion, 1994)
    Full Catastrophe Living (New York: Dell Publishing, 1990)
Thich Nhat Hanh, *The Miracle of Mindfulness* (Boston: Beacon Press, 1976)
S. Salzberg and J. Goldstein, *Insight Meditation* (workbook) (Sounds True, 2001)
Richard Moss, *The Mandala of Being* (Novato: New World Library, 2007)
Eckhart Tolle, *The Power of Now*, (Novato: New World Library, 1999)
    The New Earth, (New York: Penguin Group, 2005)

Chapter Six

Paul Pearsall, *The Heart's Code*, (New York: Broadway Books, 1998)
D. Childre and D. Rozman, *Transforming Stress*, (Oakland: New Harbinger, 2005)
    Transforming Anxiety (Oakland: New Harbinger, 2006)
    Transforming Depression, (Oakland: New Harbinger, 2007)
www.heartmath.org
J. C. Pearce, *The Death of Religion and the Rebirth of Spirit* (Rochester: Park Street Press, 2007)
Eknath Easwaran translation, *The Bhagavad Gita*, (New York: Vintage Books, 1985)
A. Harvey and K. Erickson, *Heart Yoga*, (Berkeley: North Atlantic Books, 2010)
Sharon Salzberg, *Lovingkindness*, (Boston: Shambhala, 2002)
Richard Moss, *The Mandala of Being*, (Novato: New World Library, 2007)
W. Brugh Joy, *Joy's Way*, (New York: Putnam Book, 1979)

Chapter Seven

Joan Borysenko, *Fire in the Soul*, (New York: Warner Books, 1993)
Deepak Chopra, *How To Know God*, (New York: Three Rivers Press, 2000)
Sue Monk Kidd, *When the Heart Waits* (New York: HarperCollins, 1990)
John A. Sanford, *Healing and Wholeness* (New York: Paulist Press, 1977)
Marion Woodman, *Dancing in the Flames*, (Boston: Shambhala, 1996)
www.noetic.org
www.shiftinaction.com
M. Schlitz, C. Vieten, T. Amorok, *Living Deeply*, (Oakland: New Harbinger, 2007)
Gary Zukav, *The Seat of the Soul*, (New York: Simon & Schuster, 1989)
Sharon Salzberg, *Lovingkindness*, (Boston: Shambhala, 2002)
Lynne Twist, *The Soul of Money*, (New York: W.W. Norton, 2003)
Himalayan Institute Press
www.glcoherence.org
Oriah Mountain Dreamer, *The Invitation*, (New York: HarperCollins, 1999)

www.eupsychia.com
www.holotropic.com

Epilogue

Anodea Judith, *Waking the Global Heart*, (Santa Rosa: Elite Books, 2006)
Edmund Bourne, *Global Shift,* (Oakland: New Harbinger/Noetic Books, 2008)
P. Ray, S. Anderson, *The Cultural Creatives*, (New York: Three Rivers Press, 2000)
www.thepeacealliance.org
Jacquelyn Small, *Awakening in Time*, (New York: Bantam Book, 1991)
Puran and Susanna Bair, *Living from the Heart*, (Tucson: Living Heart Media, 2009)
Andrew Harvey, *The Hope*, (New York: Hay House, Inc., 2009)

Exercises

Daily Quiet Time	Page 7
Who Am I?	Page 8
Present Moment Awareness	Page 13
Mindfulness #1	Page 14
Breath Awareness	Page 19
Diaphragmatic Breathing	Page 20
Body Awareness	Page 21
Somatic Focusing	Page 23
Journaling	Page 29
Dream Work	Page 31
Meridian Tapping	Page 41
Meditation	Page 47
Mindfulness #2	Page 49
Quick Coherence Technique	Page 56
Lovingkindness Practice	Page 57
Forgiveness Practice	Page 58
Gratitude Journal	Page 58
Heart's Desires Exercise	Page 59

About the Author

Eileen Templin, LCSW, RYT, is a licensed psychotherapist with over 25 years of counseling, training and teaching experience. She has a master's degree in clinical social work from Barry University and is a Phi Beta Kappa graduate of Penn State with bachelor degrees in social work and in religious studies.

She has taught in the Sociology and Social Work department of Lebanon Valley College and over the years has provided a variety of trainings and psychospiritual growth groups in the community. Eileen has been mentored in transpersonal psychology and in the integration of mind, body and spirit for healing and transformation.

She received her certification as a yoga teacher through the Himalayan Institute and is registered with the Yoga Alliance. Eileen's eclectic approach to therapy draws from psychodynamic, cognitive, transpersonal and energy psychology, bodily-focused psychotherapy, and the mystical traditions of the east and west. Her private practice is in Lakeland, Florida and she resides in Tampa, Florida with her husband, Steven Templin, DOM.

To learn more about Eileen visit her website at www.eileentemplin.com.

www.ingramcontent.com/pod-product-compliance
Lightning Source LLC
Chambersburg PA
CBHW081500040426
42446CB00016B/3333